AF888108

Columbia University Lectures

THE COST OF OUR NATIONAL GOVERNMENT

A STUDY IN POLITICAL PATHOLOGY

GEORGE BLUMENTHAL FOUNDATION

1909

COLUMBIA UNIVERSITY LECTURES

THE COST OF OUR NATIONAL GOVERNMENT

A STUDY IN POLITICAL PATHOLOGY

BY

HENRY JONES FORD

PROFESSOR OF POLITICS IN PRINCETON UNIVERSITY

New York

THE COLUMBIA UNIVERSITY PRESS

1910

All rights reserved

Copyright, 1910,
By THE COLUMBIA UNIVERSITY PRESS.

Set up and electrotyped. Published September, 1910.

Norwood Press
J. S. Cushing Co. — Berwick & Smith Co.
Norwood, Mass., U.S.A.

To

MY LIFE-LONG FRIEND

JOHN BLACK

OF BALTIMORE, MD.

PREFACE

THIS volume contains the substance of lectures delivered on the George Blumenthal Foundation at Columbia University in the fall and winter of 1909. The lectures were delivered from briefs, and in preparing them for publication, some documentary material cited during the argument has been transferred to foot-notes and appendices, while in other cases matter referred to but not fully quoted in the course of oral exposition, has been incorporated in the text. Oral use of statistical data is cumbersome and inconvenient, and in delivering the lectures, I referred my hearers to the forthcoming publication of them for the detailed evidence of some of my statements. The result is an inequality in the length of the lectures in their published form, but it is believed that the convenience of the reader is promoted.

I had to do with a situation that was changing while it was under consideration, and in revising the lectures I have incorporated references to pertinent events that have taken place since, when they seemed to be illustrative of the tendencies examined in the course of the lectures. The issues considered are now so acute in our politics as to make the work timely, and I hope that it will be useful in clarifying public opinion.

HENRY J. FORD.

PRINCETON UNIVERSITY,
Princeton, N.J., 1910.

CONTENTS

CHAPTER I

The Growth of Expenditure

CHAPTER II

Making the National Budget

CHAPTER III

Constitutional Agencies of Budget Control

CHAPTER IV

Theory and Practice in the United States

CHAPTER V

Some Comparisons with Other Countries

CHAPTER VI

Evolution of the American System

CHAPTER VII

Political Conditions and Tendencies

CHAPTER VIII

Possibilities of Improvement

APPENDIX A

APPENDIX B

APPENDIX C

APPENDIX D

THE COST OF OUR NATIONAL GOVERNMENT

I

THE GROWTH OF EXPENDITURE

THE rapid increase of federal expenditure is a patent fact, not disputed in any quarter. A marked feature of the situation is the criticism of it made by those in actual charge of such expenditure. This prevails to an extent that is an extraordinary manifestation in a system of party government. Ordinarily the office of accusation is left to the opposition, while the attitude of the administration is one of apology and reserve. But in the present situation we find that the sharpest and most definite accusation comes from the front rank of the party which is in charge of the government, and which, by all sound constitutional theory, is responsible for the conditions that are thus denounced. This extraordinary situation, which raises constitutional questions that we shall have to consider in their place, simplifies my task in dealing with the present topic, for I am able to cite official admissions as to the rapidity with which our national expenditure is increasing.

One of these admissions comes from Mr. George B. Cortelyou, Secretary of the Treasury under President Roosevelt. While he held that eminent position, he prepared an article on "Regulation of the National

Budget," which was published in the *North American Review* for April, 1909. This article contains the following statement: —

"The rapid growth of receipts and disbursements since the lowest point after the Civil War, and the recent tendency of disbursements to outstrip receipts, may be seen at a glance by comparing the Treasury reports at intervals of ten years as follows: —

	Net Receipts	Net Disbursements
1878	$275,446,776	$236,964,327
1888	379,266,075	259,653,959
1898	405,321,335	443,368,582
1908	601,126,118	659,196,319

"To put the comparison another way, which even more graphically illustrates the expansion: the growth in ordinary expenses for carrying on the Government, excluding interest on the public debt, but including payments for pensions and for many public works, was from $135,000,000, in 1878, to $638,000,000, in 1908 — an increase of nearly 400 per cent in a generation."

Meanwhile the increase of population — 1878 to 1908 inclusive — was less than 84 per cent.

Another of these official admissions comes from Mr. James A. Tawney, Chairman of the Committee of Appropriations of the House of Representatives. It is the custom of the chairman of the appropriations committee to give, at the close of each session, a summary of the appropriations made, with observations upon the condition of the public treasury. These reviews are full of valuable information and are worthy of greater public attention than they receive. In his review at the end of the second session of the 60th Congress,

March 4, 1909, Chairman Tawney made a startling statement in regard to the appropriations made during the session. He said: "The sum total exceeds the amount of present and prospective revenues." In his comments he remarked: —

> "In no period except in time of war have the expenditures of our National Government increased so rapidly, both in the aggregate and per capita, as these expenditures have increased during the past eight years. This fact may well cause our people not only to pause and consider the cause of this very large increase in the annual expenditures of the Government, but also to consider the necessity of checking this growing tendency towards excess."

Still another admission comes from Mr. Nelson W. Aldrich of Rhode Island, Chairman of the Senate Committee on Finance. In an elaborate speech delivered in the Senate on April 10, 1909, he said: —

> "The rapidity with which our national expenditures have increased within the last three years is a source of anxiety if not of alarm. Simultaneously with the reduction in receipts of $60,000,000 from 1907 to 1909, we have had an increase in expenditures of $120,000,000.
>
> "From an investigation more or less superficial, I am myself satisfied that the appropriations made last year could have been reduced at least $50,000,000 without impairing the efficiency of the public service. There are periods in the life of a nation when the spirit of extravagance pervades the atmosphere and the public money is scattered right and left, often without reference to the results to be secured. I hope and expect to see a radical reform in this direction."

No men can speak from more intimate knowledge than these three, the chiefs of financial administration in the executive department, in the House of Representatives, and in the Senate, respectively. It is deeply significant that their testimony, independently supplied, is in such full agreement. But note how extraordinary is the situation thus presented. The executive department, which receives the people's money, and the legislative department, which gives out the people's money, are both exhibited in an attitude of remonstrance. Where, then, does the responsibility rest? What has become of the control of the purse, which is the traditional function of the representative body? That such a situation can exist is of itself evidence that in some way constitutional government has become seriously deranged.

Senator Aldrich's opinion that the appropriations of a single year were $50,000,000 in excess of actual needs is a startling averment. The estimate seems enormous, and yet it is corroborated by the testimony of others in a position to know what is going on. So long ago as 1897, Speaker Cannon, then Chairman of the Appropriations Committee of the House, reviewing the work of the 54th Congress, in a speech delivered March 4, 1897, declared: "The appropriations are, in my judgment, in excess of the legitimate demands of the public service." Referring to Secretary Cortelyou's statement, already cited, we find that the net disbursements for 1908 exceeded those for 1898 by $215,827,737. If Chairman Cannon was correct in his opinion that the appropriations were excessive when they were so much less than they have since become, Senator Aldrich's estimate of an annual waste of $50,000,000 seems to be justified, vast as is the amount. After all, it is less than 8 per cent of the present federal expenditure, and it does not seem to be an unreasonable supposition that if a business is mismanaged and its disbursements get out of control, there may easily be a waste of 8 per cent in its expenditure. The sum is larger than the revenues of some countries of dignified position among the nations of the world — as, for instance, Switzerland, Denmark, and Norway. One of the reasons which John Milton gave for preferring republicanism to royalty was that it was more frugal; "for that the trappings of a monarchy might set up an ordinary commonwealth." But now we find that the waste of our republic would set up an ordinary kingdom. If that waste could be stopped, it would mean an enormous increase of the financial ability of the government from existing sources. The yearly application of fifty millions would carry a bond issue of over a billion and a half, which would be enough to build the Panama Canal and provide for river and harbor improvements, irrigation and reclamation works.

With expenditure exempt from control, bankruptcy is, of course, only a question of time in any business, public or private. During the second session of the 60th Congress, Senator Hale of Maine made a blunt avowal of his anticipation of national bankruptcy. He is Chairman of the Committee on Naval Affairs, and in that capacity has charge of the Naval Appropriation bill. On February 15, 1909, while that bill was under consideration, the following colloquy took place: —

"Mr. Hale. Some day, Mr. President, Congress will be confronted with the absolute, imperative, and unescapable duty and obligation either to borrow money or to increase taxes to pay the appropriations.

Mr. BACON. Is not that day right at hand?

Mr. HALE. It is too near, but it is not in the minds of men. The Senator can hardly get any votes here in this Chamber to reduce this naval programme.

Mr. TILLMAN. The Senator from Maine must think that, else he would not say it. He asserts it with such positiveness, I suppose he has made inquiry of that side.

Mr. HALE. I have made inquiry on the other side, too.

Mr. TILLMAN. I should like to cut some of these expenditures, for one.

Mr. HALE. The curtailing of expenditures is a pretty deep matter. It is more than a matter of sentiment. One man cannot do it; one committee cannot do it; one set of men cannot do it; but some day or other the Secretary of the Treasury will tell us that the money is out and there is nothing left in the Treasury; we have either got to borrow money in time of profound peace or clap on the taxes. That is coming, Mr. President, just as tides and sunrise come."

Here we have national bankruptcy declared to be the only available remedy for excessive expenditure, and the averment comes from a congressional leader who takes a prominent part in shaping and directing that expenditure. The situation is aggravated by the peculiar function which the national treasury performs under our banking system, as the agency by which coin redemption is maintained and the currency is kept at par. Hence, commerce and industry in this country are liable to distress from treasury embarrassments in ways and to extents unknown in other countries. In whatever aspect the situation may be regarded, its intense seriousness is evident.

Such are the broad outlines of the situation. The impression of unbridled extravagance which they convey is deepened when we turn to particulars. In considering them we find that expenditure tends to increase much more rapidly than population. That with the growth of the country there should be a progressive increase in government expenditure, is, of course, to be expected, although we should hardly regard any private business as well managed if the proportionate cost of operation did not decrease with the expansion of the business. We have had an enormous national development, and upon this fact a vague plea of party justification has been based for electioneering use. It is said that the reason why we have billion dollar congresses is that this is a billion dollar country. Such excuses are not approved by serious authority. In his annual review of appropriations and expenditures, delivered in the House of Representatives on May 30, 1908, Chairman Tawney gave statistics showing that, despite the great increase of population, governmental expenditure was increasing in greater proportion. The per capita expenditure has increased from $1.34, in the period from 1791 to 1796, to $8.91, in 1907. Chairman Tawney appended to his speech an analysis prepared for the Committee on Appropriations by the Bureau of the Census. This analysis is probably the most complete statement of statistical data on the subject now accessible.[1] Examination of it will correct a notion that is widely diffused, which tends to procure a leniency of public judgment that is not deserved. I refer to the notion that it is the Pension bill that makes the national expenditure seem inordinately great, so that the condition may be transitory in its nature. The statement

[1] See Appendix A.

of the Census Bureau shows that this notion is erroneous. The ratio of expense on account of pensions has declined from $4.32 to $1.92 since 1869. The marked increase of ratio is due to other costs of government.

An encouraging circumstance revealed by that analysis is that while increase of federal expenditure far outruns increase of population, it does not outrun increase of national wealth to any great extent. In the speech already mentioned, Mr. Tawney averred that federal expenditure, in comparison with national wealth, has "maintained an almost uniform proportion, except during the period of the Civil War."[1] But on referring to the Census Bureau analysis, it appears that in 1860 the federal expenditure per $1000 of national wealth was $4.40, while in 1907 it was $6.70. The statistics given in regard to expenditure by state and local authority are scantier than in the case of the federal government, but it appears that the expenditure of states, counties, cities, and minor civil divisions, amounted to $9.30 per $1000 of national wealth in 1890, and that the ratio had increased to $12.80 in 1902. This brings into view an important economic aspect of the expansion of federal functions. Evidently the transfer of function from state to federal authority is not attended by any diminution of the cost of local government, although adding to the cost of federal government. It appears that, coincident with this tendency, the cost of local government is increasing in even greater ratio than that of federal government, and that in both fields the increase is in greater proportion than the increase of national wealth. From

[1] Congressional Record for May 30, 1908, p. 7611.

this point of view there is a revelation of economic depravity in American government more impressive than is made by the absolute increase of expenditure. Federal waste is evidently but one phase of a general characteristic of American government, symptomatic of general constitutional disease. Meanwhile the steady increase of national wealth shows that the ability of the people to bear the burdens laid upon them is not seriously impaired. Great as those burdens may be, they are still far from being so great as to check the productive energies of the nation.

It is significant that this problem of budget control has become acute with the disappearance of our old state of national isolation. Contrasting our situation with that of his own nation, Mr. James Bryce, in "The American Commonwealth," says of England: —

> "She, like the Powers of the European Continent, must maintain her system of government in full efficiency for war as well as for peace, and cannot afford to let her armaments decline, her finances become disordered, the vigor of her executive authority be impaired, and sources of internal discord continue to prey upon her vitals. But America lives in a world of her own. . . . Safe from attack, safe even from menace, she hears from afar the warring cries on European races and faiths, as the gods of Epicurus listened to the murmurs of the unhappy earth spread out beneath their golden dwellings." [1]

That was published in 1888. Only twenty-one years ago, and yet what worlds away is that idyllic age! Now American banking capital is taking nations in pawn. American commercial enterprise is invading every part of the world. A boycott in China sends

[1] "American Commonwealth," Vol. I, Chap. 26.

shudders through the counting-rooms of our cotton mills, and a hurry call for relief goes to Washington. National interests naturally look to the national government for protection. That is just what government is for — to safeguard the life of the nation in all its developments. As a nation grows and as its activities expand, if its government does not respond in its functions, that is a lost nation. In becoming a world power, we are already finding that the accompanying responsibilities are subjecting our governmental organization to strains that it is unfitted to bear. These strains are bitterly deplored by our congressional politicians. The prevailing congressional opinion is that the chief cause of budget derangement is increased expenditure for national defense. It is characteristic of public events that they ignore the wishes and disregard the repose of politicians. Nations cannot choose their responsibilities, and attempts to avoid them as they present themselves only make them the harder to bear. Such experience is an incident of political evolution, and there is no escape from it. All through our history it has been the pressure of responsibility that has compelled improvement in the organization of public authority.

II

MAKING THE NATIONAL BUDGET

It is a fundamental principle of constitutional government that appropriations are made and that expenditures are controlled by the representatives of the people. Since it is officially admitted that our national representative assembly fails to discharge this constitutional function successfully, an inquiry as to the cause thereof must naturally begin with an examination of the means which it employs.

The process of budget-making starts with the transmission of a letter from the Secretary of the Treasury to the Speaker of the House of Representatives, giving estimates of appropriations required for the public service. This is a duty imposed upon the Secretary of the Treasury by law. These estimates are given in minute detail, so that when published they make a large volume. The estimates for 1910 form a quarto volume of 755 pages. On comparing them with the estimates submitted to the British Parliament, they appear to be much inferior as a source of information. The British estimates are an analytic exhibit of the various sorts of expenditure, exactly classified, even to the extent of supplying cross-references when portions of the expense of any service are carried under different headings. For instance, under the appropriations for parliamentary offices, there are references to building, stationery, and printing estimates, etc., indicating how much on parliamentary account and how much on other accounts. Moreover, the classifications are accompanied by brief explanatory comments which possess obvious utility. The estimates transmitted by the Secretary of the Treasury form simply a schedule of the demands of the various departments.

In preparing the estimates, the Secretary of the Treasury has heretofore acted in a purely ministerial capacity. In this respect important changes are taking place which will be considered later on. For the present it will be better to limit consideration to the procedure under which this growth of federal expenditure has taken place that has been officially described as great and alarming. The point to bear in mind is that heretofore the Secretary of the Treasury has had nothing to do with the budget save to transmit to the House of Representatives the estimates sent to him from the various executive departments. One will get a true idea of the function he has performed in the making of the budget if he be regarded simply as a funnel through which the departmental demands were poured upon Congress. The letter of transmission makes this point clear. In sending in the estimates for 1910, which was done on December 7, 1908, Secretary Cortelyou described them as being such as were "furnished by the several executive departments."

Until recently there has been no provision for any concert of action among the heads of the departments in preparing the estimates which they pour upon Congress through the Treasury Department funnel. All that the law has heretofore required of the heads of the several executive departments is that they shall forward their estimates to the Secretary of the Treasury on or before October 15 of each year. It then became his duty to arrange and compile the estimates thus submitted and to transmit them to Congress on the opening day of the session, together with his own estimate of the probable revenues of the government. It may seem strange that the various executive departments should act independently of one another, each formulating its own demands without any supervision or general control, but such has been the case. It is clear that this go-as-you-please method precluded anything like a systematic budget for which there is a responsible author. But, however wild and unregulated the procedure may seem to be, that has been the actual practice. Upon this point I have consulted Mr. James A. Tawney, Chairman of the Committee of Appropriations of the House of Representatives. Under date of October 13, 1909, he has given me a statement of the practice that has existed prior to March 4, 1909, when a law was passed that will be considered later on. Mr. Tawney says: —

"The head of each department prepared his estimates, or the estimates for his department, without any reference whatever to the estimates submitted by the heads of other departments, and without any reference whatever to the estimated revenues for the fiscal year for which the estimated expenditures were to be made. . . . Frequently these estimates for appropriations were far in excess of the estimated revenues. This threw upon the Committee on Appropriations the necessity of reducing the estimated expenditures so as to keep the appropriations within the estimated revenues."[1]

[1] The essential portions of Mr. Tawney's statement are given in Appendix B.

That is to say, there was nothing like team-work on the part of the executive departments. Each worked for itself. As to this, however, it should be observed that since the heads of the various departments form the President's cabinet, which meets frequently for consultation, conditions of contact and association exist that have doubtless exerted some influence upon departmental policy in all respects. But until recently no definite provision of law has existed for establishing a collective responsibility.

Congressional action on the estimates thus transmitted begins in the House of Representatives. When they are received by the Speaker, they are by him referred to the several committees having jurisdiction over particular classes of appropriations for which the estimates are made. This is done under Clause 2 of Rule 24, regulating the disposition of business on the Speaker's table. By order of this rule, unless the House itself on motion of a member directs a particular reference, the Speaker directs every executive communication to be printed and referred to the proper committee. Reference by the Speaker is the regular practice, and in the routine transaction of business the members do not know what communications have been received or how referred until they see the list published in the Congressional Record. Indeed executive communications are so numerous that no other method would be practicable. For instance, the Congressional Record for December 9, 1909, gives a list of fifty-three communications from various bureaus and departments that were referred under Clause 2 of Rule 24.

Jurisdiction over the appropriations is distributed among eight different committees of the House. The Committee on Appropriations now has charge of six of the regular appropriation bills. These are: (1) that making appropriations for legislative, executive, and judicial expenditures, (2) the District of Columbia Appropriation bill, (3) the Fortification bill, (4) the Pension bill, (5) the Sundry Civil, (6) all Deficiency Appropriation bills. The Committee on Military Affairs has charge of two of the regular appropriation bills: the Army bill and the Military Academy bill. The Foreign Affairs Committee has charge of the Diplomatic and Consular Appropriation bill. The Agricultural Committee, the Naval Committee, the Post-office Committee, the Committee on Indian Affairs, and the River and Harbor Committee have charge each of one bill with a title corresponding to that of the committee handling it. There are thirteen regular appropriation bills, and in addition there is a deficiency appropriation bill, which is quite as regular as any other bill, so that there are really fourteen regular appropriation bills, handled by eight different committees.

Thus we find in the House of Representatives a budget situation which parallels that which has heretofore existed in the executive branch — a distribution of power among separate and independent authorities, without provision for any unified control coördinating income and expenditure. It is the instinctive propensity of every executive department, and of every bureau in each department, to resist any reduction in its allotment of funds. It is the inclination of each of the special appropriation committees to resist any diminution of its share of the whole amount appropriated. Each strives to get as much as it can for the public service under its supervision. Thus there is a powerful combination of influence in favor of lavish expenditure, and there is absolutely no organized agency of control by which these expenditures under various heads may be coördinated and adjusted to income. Chairman Tawney says: "In my judgment this is one of the chief causes for the rapid increase in our appropriations for public expenditures." [1]

In addition to the estimates which are transmitted by the Secretary of the Treasury at the opening of every session, and which are known as the regular estimates, additional estimates keep pouring into the House during the session. These are known as supplemental estimates. Chairman Tawney says that this practice has been restrained by legislation aimed at it. Nevertheless supplemental estimates are still numerous every session. They are of all sorts and are sometimes for trivial amounts. The documents of the 60th Congress, 1st Session, include a supplemental estimate of $3.50 for one tire furnished for the bicycle used by a messenger of the Court of Claims.[2]

It is a curious feature of existing practice that while the Secretary of the Treasury must be notified of the cost of a bicycle tire and be the channel of communication of the Court of Claims for such an item, there is no such requirement as regards judgments rendered by the court, although they involve large amounts. Statement of these is transmitted by the Clerk of the Court

[1] See Appendix B.

[2] House Document No. 921, May 8, 1908.

in a letter to the Speaker of the House. The Court has no power to enforce its judgments, and they are not satisfied until Congress appropriates money for the purpose.

Still another class of estimates reach Congress, apart from those transmitted by the Secretary of the Treasury, either as regular or supplemental estimates; namely, the engineering estimates. An ordinary source of such estimates are investigations and surveys ordered by Congress, by means of what are known as concurrent resolutions. Their character raises a constitutional question which seems to have escaped the attention it deserves.

The Constitution provides (Art. 1, Sec. 7) that "every order, resolution, or vote, to which the concurrence of the Senate and the House of Representatives may be necessary (except on a question of adjournment) shall be presented to the President of the United States, and before the same shall take effect shall be approved by him, or being disapproved by him, shall be repassed by two-thirds of the Senate and the House of Representatives, according to the rules and limitations prescribed in the case of a bill." It is, however, assumed by Congress that a concurrent resolution is exempt from this constitutional requirement. The distinction is very fine. A joint resolution reads: "Resolved by the Senate and House of Representatives of the United States of America in Congress assembled," etc. So worded, a resolution must be presented to the President and is subject to his veto. A concurrent resolution reads: "Resolved by the Senate (the House of Representatives concurring)," etc., or else in reverse order, that body being named as the resolving party in which the resolution is offered. The form is quite unknown to the constitution and indeed seems to be in direct violation of the constitution, but it has long been established in actual practice. It is habitually employed in starting the surveys and in procuring the reports on which the appropriations made in the River and Harbor bill are based.

In addition to these classes of expenditures, the appropriation committees are expected to provide for expenditures directed by the legislation of the session. The regular estimates and the supplementary estimates are based on existing law, the engineering estimates are made in pursuance of orders of Congress previously issued. But during the session, public works, buildings, extensions of public service, enlargement of bureaus, and increases of pensions may be authorized, entailing additional expenditures. Great numbers of bills are introduced at every session proposing expenditure for various objects. These are referred to committees and from time to time omnibus bills are reported which include many separately introduced bills. Regular measures of this character are the Pension bill, the River and Harbor bill, and the Public Buildings bill. These bills are made up by a confederation of interests, — a process which, in political phraseology, is known as "log-rolling." These are bills which, because of the distribution of favors which they make among the congressional districts, are known as the "pork barrels." The term is so well established in our political nomenclature that it has been used by President Taft in public addresses.[1]

From this review it appears that there are five sources from which emanate the demands for appropriations: —

1. The regular annual estimates transmitted by the Secretary of the Treasury at the beginning of each session of Congress.

2. The supplementary estimates, also transmitted by the Secretary of the Treasury.

3. The judgments of the Court of Claims.

4. The reports of the engineers of the war department.

5. Authorization of expenditures by enactments made during the session.

Eight different committees of the House of Representatives frame and report bills granting appropriations in response to these demands. It is the practice of these committees to send for heads of departments or chiefs of bureaus, and have them explain the necessity for the appropriations for which the estimates have been transmitted. Here, again, the department heads, and indeed the different bureau chiefs of a department, may act independently in pressing the appropriations, each working to get all he can. Until recently per-

[1] The following is an extract from a speech delivered by President Taft at St. Louis, on October 26, 1909: —

"Now there is a proposition that we issue $500,000,000 or $1,000,000,000 of bonds for a waterway, and then that we just apportion part to the Mississippi and part to the Atlantic, a part to the Missouri and a part to the Ohio. I am opposed to it.

"I am opposed to it because it not only smells of the pork barrel, but it will be the pork barrel itself. Let every project stand on its bottom."

sonal solicitation of members was energetically employed, but it is declared that this practice is now discouraged.[1] It can hardly be suppressed without a radical change of system.

As a rule, the amounts carried in bills reported by the committees are below the aggregate estimates received from the five sources that have been mentioned, and they generally pass the House without extensive change. Then they go to the Senate, which works under rules that give more play to individual action than exists in the House. Under the rules of the Senate, all general appropriation bills are referred to the Committee on Appropriations, except in the case of rivers and harbors, when the reference is to the Committee on Commerce. The rules of the Senate prescribe certain formalities in regard to the insertion of new items or increases of appropriations, but it is so easy to comply with them that the appropriation bills are freely manipulated to meet the views of senators, and they are passed, loaded with amendments, to be disposed of by Committees of Conference between the two houses.[2] Senate amendment always increases the total amount of appropriations. From a statement prepared by the clerks of the Committees on Appropriations of the Senate and House, it appears that the

[1] See Appendix B.

[2] An instructive discussion of the rules of the Senate is contained in the Congressional Record, January 15, 1909, Vol. 43, No. 24, p. 964 *et seq.* The Senate has a rule that "no amendment shall be received to any General Appropriation bill, the effect of which will be to increase an appropriation already contained in the bill or to add a new item of appropriation." But it appears that the rule is subject to exceptions which empty it of any practical efficacy.

estimates for 1909 aggregated \$842,754,993.84; the appropriations, as reported to the House, aggregated \$740,220,225.47; as passed by the House, \$743,907,820.97; as reported to the Senate, \$804,298,384.79; as passed by the Senate, \$817,361,374.73; as finally enacted, \$794,614,625.80.[1] From this it appears that the appropriations, as finally determined by the Conference Committees, were increased through Senate agency over \$50,000,000 above the amount granted by the House of Representatives.

[1] Congressional Record, May 30, 1908, p. 7676.

III

CONSTITUTIONAL AGENCIES OF BUDGET CONTROL

We began our national government with a firm and precise principle of budget control; namely, that the House of Representatives held the purse-strings. It was the expectation of the framers of the Constitution that the immediate representatives of the people would control the budget and fix expenditures. The vigilant energy of the House of Commons, in asserting its exclusive right to grant supplies, was conspicuous in the politics of the times. Everybody who knew anything about public affairs knew how intense was the jealousy with which the House of Commons cherished that privilege. During the very period when public feeling in the colonies was getting excited about matters of taxation, a marked instance of this occurred. In June, 1772, when a money bill was returned to the House of Commons with an amendment by the Lords, it was at once rejected, and the Speaker tossed it over the table, whereupon it was kicked by several members on both sides.

The behavior of colonial assemblies was marked by the same spirit of jealousy as to their exclusive right to grant supplies, and it was assumed that the House of Representatives would be similarly disposed. Upon this point the strongest assurances were given to the public by men who took the lead in recommending the adoption of the Constitution. For instance, in No. 58 of *The Federalist* it is declared: —

> "The House of Representatives cannot only refuse, but they alone can propose, the supplies requisite for the support of the government. They, in a word, hold the purse — that powerful instrument by which we behold, in the history of the British constitution, an infant and humble representation of the people gradually enlarging the sphere of its activity and importance, and finally reducing, as far as it seems to have wished, all the overgrown prerogatives of the other branches of the government. This power over the purse may, in fact, be regarded as the most complete and effectual weapon with which any constitution can arm the immediate representatives of the people for obtaining a redress for every grievance and for carrying into effect every just and salutary measure."

As a matter of fact, the sole right of the House of Representatives to propose supplies was impaired by the right conferred by the Constitution upon the Senate to propose amendments. But, in contemplation of English constitutional history, the Fathers held that such was the intrinsic strength of the representative branch of the government that no check that might be applied could do more than to insure circumspect and deliberate action. That the settled will and purpose of the House could be denied was regarded as a political impossibility. The question whether the House would not be as likely to yield as the Senate, in case of a conflict, was indeed raised and considered, in this same number of *The Federalist*, and it was held that the natural preponderance of political force would be so heavily on the side of the House that both the President and the Senate would need the utmost firmness to maintain their position, even when "supported by constitutional and patriotic principles." The relation of the two houses was again considered in No. 63, with reference to legislation in general, and it was emphatically declared: —

"Against the force of the immediate representatives of the people, nothing will be able to maintain even the constitutional authority of the Senate, but such a display of enlightened policy and attachment to the public good as will divide with that branch of the legislature the affections and support of the entire body of the people themselves."

The habitual attitude of public opinion toward the Senate will hardly be described as one of affection. A Committee of the Senate in 1896 made a report deploring that "the tendency of public opinion is to disparage the Senate and depreciate its usefulness, its integrity, its power." [1] If there has been any change of tendency since, it is in the direction of increased intensity of opprobrium. And yet every session affords evidence of the ability of the Senate to override the House. An instructive instance appeared in the proceedings of the second session of the 60th Congress, ending March 4, 1909. It is not at all exceptional. Events of the same character take place during every session. But this is so typical in character and so directly pertinent to the cost of the government that it is worth considering in some detail.

The officers in charge of the Pension Bureau have been endeavoring to introduce a more simple and effective system of pension payments. According to a statement made to Congress by the Commissioner of Pensions, "more than 100 different forms of vouchers

[1] Senate Report, No. 530, 54th Congress, 1st Session.

are now required for the 18 pension agencies." If the service were consolidated in the Washington bureau, much bookkeeping and clerical work would be obviated, closer supervision of accounts could be maintained, and pensioners would be paid more promptly, as "the certificates would be issued by the bureau and mailed to the pensioners on the same date they are now mailed to the pension agency."[1] Congressional inquiry was made, hearings were given at which the Commissioner of the Interior, the Commissioner of Pensions, and other officials explained the matter,[2] and the proposed reform was approved and recommended by Committees of the House.[3] It has repeatedly passed the House of Representatives as a proviso of the Pension Appropriation bill, and the Senate has regularly amended the bill, restoring the eighteen agencies, and increasing the appropriation accordingly. On every occasion the House has submitted.

Mr. Gardner, one of the House conferees, who in March, 1909, reported a conference agreement yielding to the Senate, summed up the situation as follows: —

"Mr. Speaker, I think it is due to the House to say that for three years we have gone to the Senate with substantially the same proposition. We have met the members of the conference committees at every point, and they have never successfully met our contentions in the matter. They have said in substance, 'We do not want to and we will not concede anything; we care nothing for economy.' They say, 'We want these agencies, and we want them all.' Now, that is the ultimatum, and I might as well be plain

[1] Congressional Record, January 22, 1909, p. 1289.

[2] House Documents No. 352 and No. 785, 60th Congress, 1st Session.

[3] A full discussion of the subject is contained in the Congressional Record for January 18, 1909, pp. 1075 *et seq.*

about it. We have fought the ground over and over and over again with different conferees in three different sessions, and have come back to the House with that ultimatum every time, 'We want the agencies, and we are going to have them, and you cannot help yourselves.' That is the situation. To recede and concur means an absolute backdown on what the House has three different times said is the right position to take. The Committee, Mr. Speaker, leaves it with the House." [1]

That being the situation, Mr. Mann of Illinois held that there was nothing "left under the usage of the two bodies except for the House to recede." He remarked: —

"I think, Mr. Speaker, the conferees are entitled to the thanks of the House for the work they have done. I have always voted with the gentlemen to abolish the agencies, and I think now it is time to pass this Pension bill."

Mr. Mann's motion was agreed to without a division. The proceedings of Congress show that the Senate has ample license to pad appropriation bills according to its own will and pleasure, and that it is able to have its way, despite the protests of the House. This has been frequently admitted on the floor of the House. In 1897, Chairman (since Speaker) Cannon, in reviewing the work of the session, declared that "the General Deficiency bill, in recent sessions, as it leaves the House, providing for the legitimate deficiencies in the current appropriations for the support of the government, is transformed into a mere vehicle wherein the Senate loads up and carries through every sort of claims that should have no consideration except as independent bills reported from competent committees." [2]

[1] Congressional Record, March 4, 1909, p. 3830.

[2] Congressional Record, Vol. 29, part 3, 54th Congress, 2d Session, Appendix, p. 74.

In 1903, Chairman Cannon recurred to this matter of senatorial use of the General Deficiency bill, characterizing one item forced upon the bill by the Senate as "legislative blackmail." In reporting to the House the conference agreement reached in that bill, he remarked: —

"In May last, on the omnibus claim bill then passed, a basis was fixed for the adjustment of the accounts of Virginia and Baltimore and South Carolina with the United States, growing out of the War of 1812–1815.

"The auditing officers of the Treasury, in pursuance of that law, adjusted the accounts of Virginia. An indefinite appropriation was made to pay the respective States whatever should be found due by the auditing officers. Upon that basis and under that legislation the sum of $100,000 in round numbers has been paid to the State of Virginia.

"Under the same law, which is the law to-day, the auditing officers, in the adjustment of accounts, found due to the State of South Carolina the sum of 34 cents. Now, the Senate of the United States, notwithstanding the law to which I have referred, proposed legislation on an appropriation bill to the extent of granting to the State of South Carolina $47,000.

"The House conferees objected, and the whole long delay has been over that one item. In the House of Representatives, without criticizing either side or any individual member, we have rules, sometimes invoked by our Democratic friends and sometimes by ourselves, — each responsible to the people after all said and done, — by which a majority, right or wrong, mistaken or otherwise, can legislate.

"In another body there are no such rules. In another body legislation is had by unanimous consent. In another body an individual member of that body can rise in his place and talk for one hour, two hours, ten hours, twelve hours. It is a matter of history that a Senator on the Republican side, in a former Congress, talked to death a river and harbor bill.

"Unanimous consent comes to the center of the dome; unanimous consent comes through Statuary Hall and to the House doors, and comes practically to the House. We can have no legislation without the approval of both bodies, and one body, in my opinion, cannot legislate without unanimous consent. There was the alternative.

"In my opinion this applied not only to the Deficiency bill, but to the Naval bill. Your conferees had the alternative of submitting to legislative blackmail at the demand, in my opinion, of one individual, — I shall not say where, — or of letting these great money bills fail. Now, what are we going to do about it? This bill contains many important matters — your appropriations for public buildings, legislation lately had all along the line of public service to the extent of $20,000,000." [1]

What the House did about it was to adopt the report, carrying with it the item denounced as "blackmail."

This report in still other respects makes an interesting exhibit of the mastery of the Senate. By the terms of the agreement the Senate receded from fifteen of its amendments, while the House receded from its disagreement to 118, and in addition acceded to compromises proposed as regards four other disputed items. But even this disparity does not tell the whole story, for it is the practice of the Senate to throw in amendments for the use of the Committee of Conference in reaching an agreement, so that the concessions made by the Senate are often only mock concessions.

An exposure of this practice was once made, indirectly, but none the less completely, by the late Senator John Sherman of Ohio. The disagreements between the Senate and the House over the Tariff bill of 1894 were not settled by conference, as it was feared

[1] Congressional Record, March 3, 1903, p. 3306.

by the leaders of the House that if the measure were again brought before the Senate by a report from the Conference Committee, the report would be rejected, and the bill thus defeated. So the House passed the bill just as it came from the Senate, loaded down with amendments. Thus amendments put on in aid of senatorial strategy, and not really intended for enactment, were included in the final enactment. Senator Sherman complained that "there are many cases in the bill where the enactment was not intended by the Senate. For instance, innumerable amendments were put on by Senators on both sides of the chamber . . . to give the Committee of Conference a chance to think of the matter, and they are all adopted, whatever may be their language or the incongruity with other parts of the bill." [1]

Thus it has come about that the House, instead of being the dominant branch of the legislature, is the subordinate branch. In this respect the anticipations of the framers of the Constitution have been altogether falsified by events. As matters stand to-day, the House of Representatives is the weakest branch of the government. It has lost the power of the purse which was originally regarded as its peculiar prerogative. Instead of being strong and masterful in its relations with the Senate, as had been expected, it is abject and supine. The case becomes still more remarkable when the general characteristics of constitutional government are considered, as exhibited in the civilized world. When thus extending our view, we find that ordinarily it is the tendency of the representative assembly to

[1] Congressional Record, August 19, 1894, p. 10109.

grow in power at the expense of other branches of the government. So marked is this tendency that Professor Samuel Rawson Gardiner, the historian of the Commonwealth period in England, has formulated it as a rule of constitutional development, as follows: —

> "Once give a large constitutional place to a representative Parliament, and Parliament, merely because it is representative, will in the long run gain possession of supreme power." [1]

According to this, the characteristics of the representative branch of the government of the United States present a strange constitutional anomaly. When viewed in contrast with European representative assemblies, or with those of English commonwealths all over the world, our House of Representatives appears to be the weakest and most ineffectual national representative assembly in the world. But that statement must be qualified when the outlook is shifted to the countries south of us. Professor Gardiner's rule is a generalization from the facts of European history. It is not sustained by the facts of American history as supplied by countries south of the Dominion of Canada. Debility of representative institutions seems to be the common characteristic of the United States and the countries of Central and South America, pointing to some common influence that has deeply affected their constitutional development and has widely differentiated it from the systems upon which popular government is founded in other countries. The original constitutional tradition is, however, still sufficiently active in the House of Representatives to inspire occasional protests against the present situation. Thus some

[1] "Cromwell's Place in History," p. 88.

remarkable admissions of constitutional degeneracy have been put upon record, an example of which is the following, from a speech by Mr. Theodore E. Burton of Ohio: —

"I want to give due credit to the members of the House Committee on Appropriations for what they have done in seeking to secure economy in expenditures. What is the reason why we are deploring extravagance? The main reason is the system under which we are working, a system under which one House, charged originally with all responsibility for initiating and passing measures for raising the revenue and disbursing it, must submit their measures to another House that has unlimited authority to make additions, and has added $73,400,000 to the regular appropriation bills at this session. This is the evil in the system, that another House, with different ideas and more readily reached by those who represent local or special interests, has unlimited right to add to all appropriation bills any amount its members choose. . . .

"Under the English system the Lords do not even provide for their own clerical assistance, and it is left to the Commons to determine what they shall receive. The upper House can only reject items, or, rather, bills, in toto. The same relation is maintained between the Chamber of Deputies and the Senate in France. But here what is being done to check these large expenditures in order to bring them within reasonable limits? . . .

"Estimates are not controlled by any one responsible head, but representatives of any bureau or of any department can come here and before House committees assert their claims to larger appropriations. There is, besides, no correlation between the committee which provides the revenue and those committees which expend it. It is not to be wondered at, in this year 1908, with all these defects in our system, with the growing wealth of the country, with the demands everywhere for these extravagant expenditures, that the appropriations for the coming year should mount up to more than a billion dollars; and it is an impressive lesson to this House that we should call for a halt. (*Loud applause.*) The first place for action, as I maintain, is not to yield the prerogative of the House to the Senate. (*Applause.*)

"Let the relations between the upper House and the lower House, as they are sometimes called, be fixed, as they should be. Let this House, which is responsible to the country for the initiative of measures for revenue, be also responsible for the aggregate amount of appropriations." (*Applause.*) [1]

These remarks by Mr. Burton were made during debate on a conference committee report on the sundry civil appropriation bills. The House applauded his statements, but adopted the report.[2]

In a speech delivered in the House, June 20, 1910, Mr. T. W. Sims, of Tennessee, made the following statement: —

" I have been on the committee that handles claims on omnibus bills. In the conference I have come to an item or a claim in a bill in which I was a conferee, and when I would say that that is not a good item, that ought not to go in, it ought to go out, the answer would be, 'Oh, that is the only item that Senator So-and-so has in this bill,' and that was the only evidence of merit that was presented to the conferees very often." Congressional Record, Vol. 45, No. 159, p. 8929.

[1] Congressional Record, May 25, 1908, p. 7216.

[2] Since the above speech was made, Mr. Burton has himself become a member of the Senate. On April 15 and 16, 1910, he made an analysis of the River and Harbor bill, showing how the log-rolling system wasted the public money. He gave really startling instances. See Congressional Record, Vol. 45, No. 103, 61st Congress, 2d Session.

IV

THEORY AND PRACTICE IN THE UNITED STATES

It is a common practice to blame the Senate for the constitutional derangement now manifest in the relations of the two houses. But even if it be true, as is often alleged in these times of muck-raking literature, that the Senate has become corrupt, that does not explain its ability to override the House, for the framers of the Constitution anticipated the possibility that the Senate would become corrupt. During the debates of the Constitutional Convention, Mr. Randolph of Virginia remarked: —

"The Senate will be more likely to be corrupt than the House of Representatives, and should therefore have less to do with money matters." [1]

The truth of the matter appears to be that the Senate displays just such proclivities as the framers of the Constitution anticipated. The debates of the Constitutional Convention and contemporary literature show plainly that the Senate was expected to give special representation to wealth and social position, whereas the House should represent the masses of the people. The background of thought on this subject, in the time of the Fathers, was that supplied by the relations of the Lords and the Commons in English history. By giving special representation to wealth and social

[1] Madison's Journal, August 13, 1787.

position, the Fathers hoped to utilize for the public advantage the special knowledge, experience, and ability which wealth and social position may command. The constitutional prerogatives of the House were expected to prevent the use of senatorial influence for class advantage, and confine it to salutary operations. In this respect their expectation has been verified by the experience of other countries, but has been falsified in our republic by the breakdown of the House as an organ of control. Its actual attitude of subserviency to the Senate is contrary to the suggestions of all the political experience open to the Fathers.

Such considerations indicate that the true seat of constitutional defect is not in the Senate, but in the House. The supremacy of the Senate, now so conspicuous in our politics, is a result of the weakness and incompetency of the House. The case is simply this: Senatorial power has risen to a prodigious height because it is not held in check by the counterpoise of House authority intended by the framers of the Constitution. The cause of the wide deviation of our political practice from our constitutional theory must be sought for in the conditions under which the House transacts its business. If it be true, as has been frequently alleged in the House, that the Senate pads appropriation bills at its own will and pleasure, practising what has been described by Mr. Cannon as "blackmail," the charge implies confession of failure on the part of the House to uphold its constitutional authority. There is no escape from this conclusion. It follows that the true way to reform the Senate is to reform the House. The Senate may be brought to its proper bearings by bringing the House to its proper bearings; and it is just in this way, and in no other way, that in self-governing commonwealths throughout the world upper houses have been incapacitated from using their powers for class advantage and have been confined to an advisory function in behalf of the public welfare.

It has already been shown by citations that the deviation of our political practice from our constitutional theory is recognized and deplored in the House. It is not reasonable to suppose that leaders of the House would endure a subserviency that galls them so sorely that they complain of it bitterly, if they could help themselves. This implies that the defect is established in conditions that have grown up in the House from the circumstances in which it does business. These conditions govern and confine the activities of members. It is not fair, therefore, to attribute the failure of the House to casual defect in the personal quality of its membership. It is not the failure of any one House, or of any particular body of men who happen to form its membership. It is a continuing failure, extending back to an early period of our history. Clearly, then, the defect is not personal; it is systematic.

Such being the case, in criticizing our politics we should bear in mind a law of political phenomena laid down by Edmund Burke. In his "Thoughts on the Cause of the Present Discontents," published in 1770, he remarked: —

> "Where there is a regular scheme of operations carried on, it is the system and not any individual person who acts in it that is truly dangerous."

It is a mark of Burke's singular mental elevation and moral discernment that he was able to propound such a principle in a period when the disposition to indulge in personal accusation, that now goes by the name of muck-raking, was, perhaps, even more violent than in our own time. The muck-raking literature of that period has dropped into oblivion, but enough of it has been preserved to show that it presents a strong family likeness to that of our own time in the United States. There is a work known to students of eighteenth-century political literature, entitled "Political Disquisitions," by James Burgh. It was published in 1774, and must have had considerable circulation in the American colonies, judging from the references made to it in the writings of the Fathers. This book abounds with accusations against the statesmen of the period, including the elder Pitt, much in the style now current. There was plenty to sustain such charges, for corruption was indeed rampant. Lecky's "History of the Eighteenth Century" gives a critical account of the same conditions; and when we compare his calm and measured statements with Burgh's heated and inexact statements, we see that Burgh did not err as to the fact that corruption was prevalent, but that he mistook results for causes, and addressed his treatment to the symptoms and not to the disease. Burke drew down upon himself sharp censure because he refused to join in the popular cry of his times to turn the rascals out; but events have since shown that he was right in his diagnosis of the disease, and that its underlying cause was the existence of opportunity for the exercise of public power without public responsibility. As a matter of fact, the cleansing of English politics was brought about by change in conditions, and not by sweeping change in the personnel of the legislative body. This has been clearly pointed out by Walter Bagehot in his classic treatise on the "English Constitution." He remarks that "the statesmen who worked the system that was put up had themselves been educated under the system that was put down."

I have thought it necessary to enter into these explanations, as the system that now exists in our government cannot be explained without some reference to the situation in its personal aspects. But when I mention names, I do so simply for the purpose of illustration, and not to make any imputation upon character. Our public men are blamed for conditions that they did not create and of which they are the victims. The congresses of to-day are not inferior to the congresses of the past in the personal ability or integrity of members. Matters are not worse than they have been in the past, but the results of bad conditions are now more manifest, and the public consciousness of them is more acute and sensitive. If any one imagines there has been a golden age in our politics, if he will look for it he will not find it.

I shall now cite the case of a member of the House who in his time deservedly commanded the esteem of his constituents, and became favorably known to the nation at large because of his vigilant activity. He was widely known as the "watch-dog of the Treasury." I refer to the late Judge Holman of Indiana. Under the title "Something of Men I have Known," the Hon. Adlai E. Stevenson, Vice-President of the United

States during President Cleveland's second term, has published a book of reminiscences. It contains the following anecdote of Judge Holman : —

"It has been said that even great men have at times their weaknesses. An incident to be related will possibly show that Judge Holman was no exception to that rule. The consideration of sundry bills for the erection of post-office buildings in a number of districts, having 'gone over' by reason of his objection, the members having the bills in charge joined forces and jumped the several measures into an 'omnibus bill' which was duly presented. The members especially interested in its passage, to make assurance doubly sure, had quietly inserted a provision for the erection of a Government building in one of the cities of Holman's district.

"When the bill was read, Judge Holman, as he sat busily writing at his desk, was, without solicitation on his part, the closely observed of every member. Apparently oblivious, however, to all that was occurring, he continued to write. No objection being made, the bill was in the very act of passing, when a member from Wisconsin rushed to the front and exclaimed : —

"'Mr. Speaker, I desire to call the attention of the gentleman of the Fourth district of Indiana to the fact that the Treasury is being robbed!' Unmoved by the appeal, the Judge continued to write, and, as one of his colleagues afterward remarked, 'was chewing his tobacco very fine.' After a moment of suspense, and amid applause, in which even the galleries took part, the member from Wisconsin in tragic tones exclaimed : —

"'Ah, Mr. Speaker, our watch-dog of the Treasury, like all other good watch-dogs, never barks when his friends are around!'"

Here we have an instance of the dilemma in which every member of Congress continually finds himself. What should Holman have done? He might have affronted interests on whose help he depended for his seat. He might have sacrificed himself, and Congress would have lost the advantage of his laborious and useful activity. But what he might have been unwilling to do, other candidates in his district would have been eager to undertake. As Edmund Burke wisely said, "Whatever is the road to power, that is the road which will be trod."

But this is not all. Had he scorned the sop offered to shut his mouth, he would not only have rejected a district favor, but he would have antagonized the interests of other districts, and thus have diminished his ability to serve his constituents in other respects, or indeed to exert any positive influence upon legislation. The conditions are such that members are practically dependent upon the aid and good-will of their fellow-members for the chance of obtaining any consideration whatever for a legislative proposal, however meritorious.

During the sessions of Congress bills pour in at an average rate of more than 150 a day. This torrent swells with every legislative session,[1] and in the 59th

[1] A report from the Superintendent of the House document room (House Document No. 704, 60th Congress, 1st Session) gives the following statistics of congressional documents, omitting resolutions and treaties: —

Congress	House Bills	Senate Bills	House Reports	Senate Reports	House Documents	Senate Documents	Public Laws	Private Laws
Fifty-fourth	10,378	3,736	3,080	1,575	786	503	434	514
Fifty-fifth	12,223	5,594	2,367	1,893	1,000	711	551	885
Fifty-sixth	14,399	6,070	3,006	2,496	1,316	694	443	1,499
Fifty-seventh	17,560	7,447	3,919	3,318	1,213	680	480	2,310
Fifth-eighth	19,209	7,295	4,904	4,402	1,319	536	575	3,467
Fifty-ninth	25,897	8,627	8,174	7,342	1,745	949	774	6,249

Redlich, in his "Procedure of the House of Commons" (Vol. III, p. 282), gives statistics as to legislation from 1890 to 1903. The public bills introduced in the House of Commons ranged from 384 in 1890 to 311 in 1903. The private bills ranged from 125 in 1898 to 116 in 1903. The public bills sent down by the House of Lords ranged from 8 to 21 in the course of a session; private bills, from 82 to 113.

Congress aggregated over 34,000. It is a physical impossibility to give them consideration. An instructive analysis of the situation was made by Mr. Martin E. Olmsted, in a speech delivered in the House on January 7, 1909.[1] He remarked: —

"We have upon this floor 391 members and enough delegates to make in round numbers 400. Knock off a few thousand bills, and for convenience call it 30,000. If we allow an average of one minute for each of the 400 members to debate each of the 30,000 bills, that would allow for debate alone 12,000,000 minutes, or 200,000 hours, equal to 20,000 days of 10 hours each. Allow 300 working days to the year, and we have $66\frac{2}{3}$ years as the requisite time for debate of the pending business. The reading of the bills, roll-calls, etc., would carry us beyond threescore and ten, the alloted life of man. But the life of a Congress is only two years."

It is therefore a physical impossibility for the House to get through its business by proceeding in regular order through the calendars. But a complex system of rules has been evolved by which the mass may be winnowed. Bills for raising revenue, general appropriation bills, and bills for the improvement of rivers and harbors are given precedence. The presentation of a report from a committee of conference is always in order. A report from the Committee on Rules is always in order, and no dilatory motion may be entertained until it is disposed of. By means of such privileged motions, interests controlling the Committee on Rules can always bring up for consideration any measure they deem of sufficient importance. The rules also provide means for privileging the consideration of other bills, provided a sufficient number of members combine for the purpose. On the first and

[1] Congressional Record, Vol. 43, No. 17, p. 611 *et seq.*

third Mondays of the month any bill may be taken up and passed out of its regular order, whether or not it has been considered by a committee, if the rules be suspended by a vote of two thirds of the members voting, in which case debate is limited to 40 minutes. By an amendment to the House rules, adopted in March, 1909, members may have bills that have been favorably reported placed on a special calendar, known as the "Calendar of Unanimous Consent," and on days when it shall be in order to suspend the rules, this calendar is to be taken up immediately after the approval of the Journal. A single objection will not only prevent consideration of the bill, but will also cause it to be stricken from this calendar.

The circumstances are such that the only available method of getting bills through is for members to help one another, or, to use the common term, by log-rolling. The term is a metaphor drawn from pioneer life. It refers to the custom by which all the neighbors lent a hand to roll the logs when a man was putting up a cabin. Log-rolling is a practice characteristic of all American legislative bodies. It is an ancient practice. By means of it Congress and our state legislatures hustle through a vast quantity of business. This practice has been much censured. It undoubtedly produces crude and excessive legislation. The output is not the expression of the knowledge and judgment of members, but of their mutual tolerance and indulgence. Often the mass of the members may not really know what is going on. In state legislatures it is a common practice for recording clerks to enter the names of members as voting for measures, unless expressly notified to the contrary. Nevertheless, under the conditions which exist in American legislative bodies, log-rolling is the only way in which the ordinary member may hope to obtain consideration for any measure he may introduce.

It is easy to see how log-rolling enlarges senatorial opportunity. The members of the Senate, being fewer in number, have more individual time, and under the elastic rules of the Senate they have almost unlimited powers of individual action. Hence they are much stronger in rolling logs than the members of the House, and these habitually turn to them for assistance. In padding appropriation bills senators are operating for members of the House as well as for themselves. They are in a position to punish opponents as well as reward adherents. Hence in a conflict they can count upon strong support in the House. Therefore, while the House always applauds declarations of its constitutional rights, it always surrenders them in practice.[1] Immediately after the speech of Mr. Burton, cited in the preceding lecture, he was asked by a member how he proposed to establish budget control by the House. The following colloquy then took place: —

"Mr. Burton of Ohio. I think the more appropriate way is for the House to insist on its prerogatives, and especially that no member of the House, when he is disappointed about an appropriation, shall go over to the Senate and have it tacked on there. That is one of the beginnings of extravagance.

"Mr. Clark of Missouri. That will be done when human nature has been entirely remodeled." [2]

[1] The right of the Senate to originate special appropriation bills has been explicitly conceded by the House. See House Reports, No. 147, 46th Congress, 3d Session.

[2] Congressional Record, May 25, 1908, p. 7216.

This reveals the secret of House subserviency. It is an outcome of the log-rolling system of legislation, and cannot be cured while that system endures.

With the transfer to the Senate of budget control goes its correlated power, — legislative control. By its ability to manipulate the "pork-barrel" bills, the Senate can put great pressure on the House. This means of controlling the actions of the House was clearly exposed in the struggle over the Emergency Currency bill in May, 1908. The state of sentiment in the House was strongly adverse to the bill, as shaped by the Senate. In this situation Mr. Richard Bartholdt of Missouri, Chairman of the Public Buildings Committee, gave out for publication the following announcement: —

"I served notice on the Speaker to-day that I would not call up the conference report on the Public Buildings bill until a satisfactory currency bill has been passed. The conferees on this bill have reached a final agreement, and their report has been adopted by the Senate. I told the Speaker that my constituents, especially Republicans, are urging on me with much vigor the absolute necessity of enacting at this session the emergency currency measure, and that I agreed with them, and I believe, with a majority of the thinking people of the country, that such legislation is necessary to restore confidence and guard against recurrence of panic conditions.

"The situation is this: the country is looking to the Republican party to pass an emergency currency bill. Congress has been in session six months, and has failed to agree on a currency measure. If we adjourn without doing anything more than creating a currency commission, it will be up to the Republican party to make embarrassing excuses if panic conditions recur this fall. Furthermore, a Presidential campaign approaches.

"I have the report of the conference on the Public Buildings bill in my pocket. I am going to keep it there until a satisfactory currency bill is passed. The House and Senate conferees on currency are at the threshold of a tentative compromise. There is no reason why we should not enact their agreement into law. I, for one, am willing to stay here all summer, if it is necessary, to 'starve out' any recalcitrant group or faction." [1]

Subsequently, in debate in the House, Mr. Bartholdt justified his action on the ground that it was necessary in order to keep a quorum of members in attendance. He said: "At least a hundred members of this House have come to me during the last ten days and stated that if it was not for this Public Buildings bill they would have to go home, because other important business was hardly to be expected." Hence he held back the Conference Committee report until the Emergency Currency bill was passed. An agreement between the Senate and House conferees on the Public Buildings bill was reached on May 23. It was not presented to the House until May 30. A schedule of the changes acceded to by the House conferees occupies seven columns of the Congressional Record. In presenting the report, Chairman Bartholdt explained: "The House yielded to the individual demands of senators which were embodied as Senate amendments for building facilities in their respective states." [2] This admission of subserviency provoked no comment. Only four nays were recorded in opposition to the adoption of the report.

It therefore appears that the final outcome of the methods employed by the House is the destruction not only of its budget control, but also of its legislative

[1] The transaction is described in Congressional Record, May 30, 1908, pp. 7629, 7690 *et seq.*

[2] Congressional Record, May 30, 1908, p. 7689.

control. The real legislative chamber is the Committee of Conference, in which the Senate has the mastery.[1]

Thus the conditions under which the House does business destroy its liberty of action, and it is subjected to the rule of interests that are in a position to avail themselves of the complications of the committee system. That rule is odious, but it is irresistible so long as the conditions which promote it continue to exist. The results which we are now witnessing exactly conform to the prophecy of Alexander Hamilton, in describing the consequences which manifest themselves when legislative action is not guarded by institutions that subordinate particular interests to the general interest. He said: —

"The public business must, in some way or other, go forward. If a pertinacious minority can control the opinion of a majority respecting the best mode of conducting it, the majority, in order that something may be done, must conform to the views of the minority; and thus the sense of the smaller number will overrule that of the greater and give a tone to the national proceedings. Hence, tedious delays; continual negotiation and intrigue; contemptible compromises of the public good." [2]

[1] In a brief speech delivered in the House, May 13, 1884, Mr. John Sherman of Ohio said: —

"We have by our practice heretofore gradually extended the powers of Committee of Conference, until now a proposition to send a bill to conference startles me when I remember what occurred in the Committee of Conference on the tariff bill last year. I feel that both houses ought to make a stand on the attempt to transfer the entire legislative power of Congress to a committee of three of each body, selected not according to any fixed rule, but probably according to the favor of the presiding officer or the chairman of the committee that framed the bill; so that, in fact, a committee selected by two men, one in each House, may frame and pass the most important legislation of Congress."

[2] *The Federalist*, No. 22.

V

SOME COMPARISONS WITH OTHER COUNTRIES

CONGRESS habitually disclaims responsibility for the results of the methods it employs. Responsibility is shifted from the House to the Senate, or from Congress to the Executive, or even to the mass of the people, which is a convenient place to put it, for if the people themselves are to blame, they have no right to find fault with their representatives. In reviewing the appropriations of the first session of the 60th Congress, Chairman Tawney said : —

"The responsibility of the House of Representatives in respect to the appropriation of money from the federal treasury is a direct responsibility we owe to the people. It is a non-partisan responsibility."

This view of the case is emphasized in the head-lines which he supplied to his speech as published in the Congressional Record.[1] They include this averment : —

"The Insistent Demands of the People and of the Public Service Result in an Increased Aggregate."

In his review at the close of the second session of the same Congress, Chairman Tawney again laid the responsibility on the people themselves. After declaring that the sum total of the appropriations of the session "exceeds the amount of present and prospective revenues," he said : —

[1] Congressional Record, Vol. 42, No. 138, May 30, 1908, p. 7609.

"The great increase in expenditures is attributable to insistent Executive recommendations and a misguided public demand for the inauguration and execution of new projects without a due realization of the consequent charges." [1]

At the close of the same session Mr. Hemenway, of Indiana, a member of the Senate Committee on Appropriations, made a statement offering the same argument in favor of a release from responsibility. He contrasted estimates with appropriations actually made, and he figured that in the last seven years Congress had reduced the estimates of the executive departments by an aggregate amount of $274,000,000. In concluding his remarks, he observed: —

"I invite the attention of the country to this table. It shows the facts, and although the estimates were not reduced to the extent many of us wanted, Congress has not added to its popularity with the people by the reductions it did make, for on the whole the people have been with the Executive in urging that all recommendations of the Executive be carried out." [2]

These pleas appeared at a time when it is the practice to put matter in the Congressional Record for campaign use, and obviously they were meant as excuses by the majority party in Congress. Thus it appears that congressional responsibility is transferred to the executive department, and then that is exonerated on the ground that it has been responsive to the desires of the people. It follows that if the situation is to be amended, the people must themselves say what shall be done. The logic of much congressional utterance is like that of a physician who might tell a patient,

[1] Congressional Record, Vol. 43, No. 69, March 4, 1909, p. 3913.
[2] Congressional Record, March 3, 1909.

"All that you have to do is to say what you want me to give you, and I will gladly write the prescription."

The practice of the opposition is to put the blame on the party in power, despite the fact that members of all parties coöperate in passing the "pork-barrel" bills. Senator Tillman of South Carolina, who is blunt of speech, has declared that when general stealing is going on, it is his business to see that his state gets its share. In the course of Senate debate he candidly declared: "The whole scheme of river improvement is a humbug and a steal; but if you are going to steal, let us divide it out, and not go on complaining." [1] When the naval appropriation bill was before the Senate in 1899, he remarked: "We have a little orphan of a naval station down in South Carolina, for which I am trying to get a few crumbs of this money which is being wasted." [2]

But when Senator Tillman gets what he has described as his share of the steal, that does not prevent him from censuring the administration for extravagance; and, in general, while members of the minority take as large a hand in the grab game as they can, they do not acknowledge any responsibility for the results. The fact that they help to produce these results is too

[1] Congressional Record, March 4, 1901, p. 3906.

[2] In this effort Senator Tillman has been remarkably successful. During debate in the Naval Appropriation bill in 1909, a tabulated statement of navy-yard expenditure was presented, from which it appears that in the six years, 1902–1907, inclusive, the expenditure upon the Charleston Navy Yard aggregated $2,592,829.30. During that time no use at all was made of the yard for naval purposes, and the value of the work done is officially returned as "None." See Congressional Record, Vol. 43, No. 55, February 17, 1909, p. 2616.

patent to be denied by any respectable apologist, but it is contended that their participation is not such as to incur responsibility.

At the close of the first session of the 60th Congress, Mr. Fitzgerald of New York made a statement in behalf of the Democratic members of the Committee on Appropriations, in which he said: —

"I challenge the Chairman of the Committee on Appropriations now, and I shall yield to him to answer, to name a single item of large appropriation where the Record does not show more Democrats recorded against it than there are Republicans recorded against it. (*A pause.*) The gentleman does not care to answer. I make the assertion that in every instance when his committee was overridden, or when appropriations were improperly enlarged, more Republicans voted the reckless appropriation than did the Democrats, and more Republicans in proportion to their numbers in this House than Democrats. With a majority of fifty-seven members in this House it is a pitiable spectacle for the Chairman of the great Committee on Appropriations to have to plead that the majority of fifty-seven was unable to prevent the minority from looting the Treasury." [1]

Thus it appears that no matter what the connection of congressional factions with the process may be, there is a common determination to avoid responsibility for results. In the transfer of responsibility which goes on, that which selects the executive department as the scapegoat seems to be peculiarly audacious, in view of the way in which congressional procedure confines executive management. No business principle is better established than that, in order to be responsible for results, an agent must have control of means. Congress habitually violates this principle. The Post-

[1] Congressional Record, Vol. 42, No. 138, May 30, 1908, p. 7613.

office Department is a striking instance of this. It is the rule in other countries that the post-office is a source of public profit. In the United States, while rendering service less in extent and in quality, the post-office is a sink-hole of public money. In the United Kingdom, the postal service in 1907 yielded a surplus of over $25,000,000. In that year the operations of our Post-office Department showed a deficit of $8,587,361, which increased to $13,664,108 in 1908. In the decade 1899–1908 the total deficit of our Post-office Department has aggregated $87,644,188, although the receipts increased from $95,021,384 to $191,478,663 per annum. In Canada, with much smaller population and yet with an area about equal to that of the United States, the Post-office Department is operated with profit at lower rates for service in some respects than in the United States. The inferiority of our postal service is notorious. Every postmaster-general labors to improve it, but he finds the way barred. Incredible as the statement may seem, the Post-office Department is not ordinarily consulted as to the location of the buildings which form its business plant. Postmaster-General Meyer, in his report for 1908, mentions that appropriations aggregating $18,000,000 had been made for post-office buildings the previous year, but that the department had had nothing to do with the selection of sites. In order to assure myself on this point, I wrote to Mr. Meyer, and was informed that at the previous session more than $20,000,000 had been appropriated without any recommendation from the department.[1]

[1] See Appendix C. The disregard of economy involved by the process is illustrated by the following statement, made by Senator Clay of Georgia: —

A curious feature of post-office management, as thus restricted by Congress, is the situation that now exists with respect to the parcels post. Efforts of department officials to induce Congress to permit the extension of that branch of the service have been baffled for many years. Restriction upon this class of business is a great cause of the heavy loss incurred in rural mail delivery. But facilities which Congress denies to the American people in their own country have been obtained for them in other countries by executive arrangements. While parcels over four pounds in weight (except single books) are excluded from domestic mails, the limit is raised to eleven pounds for parcels with a foreign destination. Hence one may send a parcel weighing eleven pounds to any foreign country in the postal union (which includes 38 countries), while the same mails which carry that parcel will reject any parcel over four pounds (not a single book) addressed to a place in the United States, even if only a few miles away from the point of origin. The rate is 16 cents a pound for domestic mails, and only 12 cents for foreign mails. From an economic point of view the situation is singularly fatuous. Unremunerative long-haul business is being preferred to profitable short-haul business.

A like predominance of particular interest over the general welfare is visible in naval administration. The

"I heard evidence the other day that demonstrated to my mind that we paid $50,000 for the construction of a building in a town where the rent for the building theretofore used was $250 per year, and after the new building was constructed the services of a janitor cost $600 per year." Congressional Record, Vol. 45, No. 132, May 20, 1910, p. 6803.

executive department has been trying to induce Congress to permit a concentration of dock-yard equipment, to reduce expenditure and increase efficiency. But Congress is disposed to retain navy yards as a favor to localities, even when they are too small to be useful. Local interests are so much more important than general interests in the minds of members, that actually it has been contended on the floor of the Senate that instead of having navy yards to suit the navy, the navy should be made to suit the navy yards, and thus justify the millions spent upon them, which now goes to waste. During a debate on the Naval Appropriation bill, of which Senator Hale has charge, he was accused of advocating the maintenance of navy yards incapable of docking a modern battleship. In reply he said: —

"What does the senator expect? — that navy yards which have been dealing with smaller ships can be equal to the new and larger ships? That is one of the arguments that was used against these enormous ships — that they can get into only two or three yards. But is that the fault of the navy yards?"

Senator Hale referred to this complaint about useless navy yards as "an indictment against the folly of Congress in ordering these monsters," meaning our modern war-ships. Later on he indicated his solution of the difficulty. He said, "I am in favor of smaller ships." [1]

Please observe that I am not making any imputation upon Senator Hale's character. I cite the affair simply as a typical instance of the way in which legislative segmentation and control through standing

[1] Congressional Record, Vol. 43, No. 53, February 15, 1909, p. 2435.

committees, enable local interests to subordinate the national welfare. The same disposition is exhibited in the English Parliament. President Lowell of Harvard, in his work on "The Government of England," says: —

> "The members of the half-dozen boroughs where the state maintains great shops for the construction and repair of war-ships are always urging the interests of the workmen; and they do it with so little regard to the national finances, or to the question whether they are elected as supporters or opponents of the ministry, that they have become a byword in Parliament under the name of 'dock-yard members.'"[1]

So you see that the same influences that are at work in our Congress are at work in the English Parliament, but with this vast difference, that under our committee system the dock-yard members have charge of the naval appropriations, while in England the administration has charge of them.

Congressional pretenses to the effect that the appropriations are made in pursuance of executive recommendations are not sustained by the facts as exhibited in congressional procedure. The executive department has not been allowed to have anything to do with budget-making in a responsible way. The appropriation bills take their shape from the views and interests of localities. National policy, as expressed in the recommendations of the executive department, is continually thwarted or ignored. And yet this disposition manifested in Congress to put upon the executive department the responsibility for results which it is powerless to prevent, and which are contrary to its

[1] Vol. I, p. 149.

desire, reflects a sound constitutional tradition. That is where the responsibility ought to rest, and the only cure for the present state of constitutional disease is to put that responsibility wholly upon the executive department. It is just here that the fundamental difference exists between our republic and the other commonwealths that have sprung from the English constitutional stock. Under the English constitutional system, no appropriation can be voted unless the administration accepts responsibility for it by a specific recommendation.

The rule of order of the House of Commons governing this matter dates back to July 11, 1713. It is now the oldest of the standing orders of the House of Commons. It runs as follows: —

> "This House will receive no petition for any sum relating to public service, or proceed upon any motion for a grant or charge upon the public revenue . . . unless recommended by the Crown."

This rule is construed as prohibiting any motion to insert an item in an appropriation bill, or to increase any item beyond what has been asked by the government. A similar provision appears in every constitution of British make, so that it may be regarded as the English constitution hall-mark. Here is the way in which it appears in the constitution granted to the Dominion of Canada in 1867: —

> "It shall not be lawful for the House of Commons to adopt or pass any Vote, Resolution, Address, or Bill for the appropriation of any part of the Public Revenue, or of any Tax or Impost, to any purpose, that has not been first recommended to that House by message of the Governor-General in the Session in which such Vote, Resolution, Address, or Bill is proposed."

This provision is the great antiseptic of the English constitution. It absolutely precludes log-rolling, and in so doing dries up the most copious source of legislative graft. It establishes the representative assembly in its proper function as an organ of control. This explains the great jealousy with which the Commons cherish their exclusive prerogative of budget-making. When they themselves are so fixed that they cannot indulge motives of private favor and privilege, they take good care that such opportunity does not exist elsewhere. Thus in any conflict between the chambers the members stand together, and the collective might of the House is pitted against the prerogative of the Lords.

The principle of executive responsibility in budget-making is not peculiar to the English system. It is the foundation of responsible government wherever it exists. When English example is cited in our Congress, it is the fashion to reply that such procedure is an incident of monarchical rule and cannot be applied to our system. But we find the same system in Switzerland, still more drastically applied. Switzerland is a federal republic like our own. It is a union of sovereign states. The Swiss constitution explicitly declares that "the cantons are sovereign." The Federal Assembly, corresponding to our Congress, is declared by the constitution to be "the supreme authority." All legislative authority is concentrated in it, and among its powers is expressly mentioned "the determination of the budget." But in actual practice the executive department prepares the budget and proposes all measures of taxation, including long and elaborate tariffs. More than that, so intense is the determination of the Swiss Congress to keep itself in a position to control and supervise, that it will not consider any bill unless it has first been referred to the executive department for examination and report.[1]

Wherever the preparation of the budget is not an executive duty, signs of constitutional derangement appear. While nowhere else in the world is found any parallel to the powers which our Senate exercises in levying taxes and making appropriations, there are countries in which log-rolling practices prevail, — notably in France, Italy, Spain, and Portugal, — and in them we find that the procedure subjects the budget to the manipulation of particular interests. The budget is submitted by the government, but is exposed to committee manipulation, and opportunities exist for action in behalf of private interests at the expense of public interests. Representative institutions do not necessarily secure responsible government. The natural tendency, exhibited everywhere and always, so far as circumstances permit, is for those in the representative position to use their opportunities for themselves. Unless efficient means of counteracting this tendency are provided, representative institutions are converted into agencies of class advantage and private profit. Signs of constitutional decay from this cause are visible in countries that have adopted parliamentary institutions without the English budget safeguards.

I have been asked how the cost of our government

[1] "The Swiss Confederation," by Adams and Cunningham, p. 47. The work is authoritative. It was prepared with the aid of Swiss publicists.

compares with that of other countries. After much consideration, I am convinced that it is impossible to answer that question. It is easy to compare disbursements, and comparisons of this sort are frequently made for electioneering use. The annual volumes of the Statistical Abstract, issued by the Bureau of Statistics at Washington, contain tables showing expenditures per capita. It appears that in 1907 the per capita expenditure of the federal government was only $6.73, while in some other countries it was far greater. A per capita calculation, including the principal nations, is given in the Statesman's Year Book for 1909. In this also the per capita expenditure of the United States appears much less than that of most other nations, although far in excess of Turkey and China. If small per capita expenditure be the mark of good government, the palm must be given to China, for according to this tabulation its per capita expenditure is put at 8 pence as against 1*l.* 12*s.* 6*d.* for the United States, and 3*l.* 8*s.* 2*d.* for the United Kingdom. But while giving these figures, the Statesman's Year Book is careful to say that they have no comparative value, for reasons thus stated: "Revenue and expenditure, which in some states are raised and expended by local authorities, are in others included in the national accounts; debt in some countries is incurred merely for the sake of profitable investment, while in others it is unproductive and burdensome; in some states the creditors are citizens, while in others they are foreigners; debt charges generally include more or less amortization, but sometimes only the interest is stated."

But even if statistical analysis could be extended to

all these factors, a comparative statement of the cost of government in different countries would be still impossible, for while outlay might be computed, the returns could not be. It may happen that, while public expenditure is increased, the aggregate may be far less than the private expenditure abolished. For instance, the claim is made by New Zealand authorities that passenger and freight rates on the state railroads are the lowest in the world. While on a visit to this country, Sir Joseph G. Ward, the New Zealand premier, said that "when our railroads produce 3 or 3½ per cent, we make large concessions on passenger and freight rates." The effect of this policy is a great reduction of shipping costs, of which the people get the benefit. In New Zealand the disbursements of the government in 1908 were over $40,000,000 for a population of less than a million citizens, the per capita being over $40. It is clear in this case that high per capita is an evidence of high function, while such low per capita as appears in the case of Turkey and China is evidence of low function.

The truth of the matter appears to be that everywhere the democratizing of governmental function is accompanied by a process of transfer of social costs from private to public account. Whether or not results will be salutary or pernicious depends upon the degree of administrative efficiency. Just as in the case of private business, it is not the amount of the investment that determines the result, but the skill with which it is applied and managed. Enterprises which in one country may be profitable may in another be burdensome. The strong tendencies everywhere manifest to augment the administrative tasks of government introduce conditions which will try the souls of nations. The state, like every organism, must have power to adjust its activities to the conditions of its being, or else it is doomed. The strains to which modern nations are now subjected will have consequences that will doubtless produce new groupings of empire. Probably by the end even of the present century the map of the world will look very different from what it does now.

VI

EVOLUTION OF THE AMERICAN SYSTEM

When viewed from the standpoint of comparative politics, American politics seem to be characterized by extreme irrationality. In every other civilized country the constitution provides means by which the administration can formulate its policy, propose measures to the legislature, and bring them to determination. This is the simple and rational order which is found in sound corporate management of every kind, large or small. Any one would be regarded as crazy who should seriously propose that the president of a company ought not to attend meetings of the directors, or that he ought not to have the right to prepare business for their consideration. But just such arrangements pervade the organization of public business in all spheres of government in the United States. It seems to be the quintessence of absurdity that the people should be put continually to great expense and effort to elect presidents, governors, and mayors, as exponents of public policy, when, after all, those elected are not to have the opportunity of formulating public policy. It is going through a great deal to arrive at nothing definite or conclusive.

The remarkable thing is not that the system breeds corruption, but that it should work at all. Any one who will consider what would happen if such arrangements as exist in public business were applied to private business, will readily comprehend why graft pervades American politics. Fancy a railroad president trying to run his lines successfully while excluded from the directors' meetings at which allotments of funds and equipment are determined. No business man would expect anything else than that systematic jobbery would be the inevitable result. And yet the management of public business in the United States is subject to just such conditions. It follows that extravagance, corruption, and graft are not adventitious in the American system of government; they are its natural concomitants.

This raises the problem: How did the United States acquire such a system? Certainly not by inheritance, for its characteristics are the reverse of those which appear in all other offshoots of the English constitutional stem. If the fact were not historically evident, no one could imagine that the governmental methods of the United States had any ancestry in common with those of the United Kingdom, the Dominion of Canada, and the Commonwealth of Australia. What, then, has been the cause of the great divergence in development? The case propounds an important problem to political science, but it is one that admits of ready solution, for in tracing back the divergence to its beginnings it appears that it originated in the separation of the executive department from the legislature. This is the peculiarity of the American system, which differentiates it from that of all other countries save those of Central and South America. If our House of Representatives is weak and ineffectual as compared with other representative assemblies, it is also the case that our House of Representatives differs from all its congeners in that it lacks the presence of the Executive to add to its importance and enhance its prestige. During the controversy between the House of Representatives and President Roosevelt as to the supply of funds for the secret service, congressional leaders complained of their inability to reach the public ear with a statement of their side of the case. The fact was deplored that the conspicuous position occupied by the President gave a range to his utterance with which Congress could not compete.[1] But it is clear that if the executive forum had been in the House itself, executive averment and the response thereto would have occupied a common center of interest, and it would have been impossible to focus observation upon the one without taking in the other.

The peculiar privation which our House of Representatives experiences was inflicted upon it by a doctrine that was powerfully influential during the period in which the United States began its career as an independent nation. It is the doctrine commonly known as the separation of the powers. In the form in which it became famous it was promulgated by the eighteenth-century French publicist, Montesquieu. It

[1] A resolution was offered in the House to print for distribution 2,000,000 copies of the report of the proceedings of the House in reply to the President's charges, but it was defeated. In the course of debate, on January 14, 1909, Mr. Williams, the minority leader, said, "We knew when we took up the cudgels that the President threw down that he could get the ear of the country for a message, and that we could not get the ear of the country for speeches made in opposition."

is contained in Book XI of his "Spirit of the Laws," published in 1748.

At present this doctrine survives only in the United States and the Spanish-American republics. It is dead everywhere else. France (1791) and Norway (1814) both adopted it in their national constitutions, but both after violent struggle and distress rejected it. In the eyes of European publicists it now possesses merely an antiquarian interest. Even such a voluminous work as the "Cambridge Modern History" curtly dismisses it as "an illusory theory" and as an "hallucination" that hindered the formation of agencies for the control of government by public opinion.[1]

At the time it was formulated, however, it met with an enthusiastic reception in England. At that time reformers were struggling to find means of counteracting the personal will of the monarch without impairing the public value of his office. This was eventually accomplished by arrangements giving the custody of Crown authority to a prime minister raised to power by the representatives of the people. If one is able to look through appearances into realities, it will be seen that in all English-speaking commonwealths the purport of a general election is the choice of a President; the essential difference lies in the way the President is treated after he is elected. By so much as his power of initiative is abridged, the sovereignty of the people is impaired. But in the eighteenth century the possibility of such a transfer of power from the basis of prerogative to the basis of popular control was not comprehended, and the aim proposed by reformers

[1] "Cambridge Modern History," Vol. VI, p. 811.

was to confine prerogative. It became the fashion to praise Montesquieu's theory of the English constitution, and from England the doctrine passed into the American colonies. In England its influence was exhausted in producing a transient phase of opinion; in America it was speedily translated into practice in the course of the constitution-making to which the states were committed as a result of the Revolution. The principle of the separation of the powers was explicitly recognized in six of the twelve state constitutions adopted prior to 1787, and enunciation of that doctrine has been a general characteristic of American state constitutions ever since. The Constitution of the United States is, however, a remarkable exception, for it does not contain any enunciation of that principle. The omission could not have been the result of inadvertence, as the framers of the Constitution diligently consulted the text of existing state constitutions, and had before them distinct assertions of that principle. The constitution of Maryland, adopted in 1776, declared that "the legislative, executive, and judicial powers of government ought to be forever separate and distinct from each other." The Massachusetts constitution of 1780 asserts the same principle with more emphasis. Any such declaration is conspicuously absent from the federal Constitution. Moreover its provisions violate that principle, which indeed was one of the objections raised to the adoption of the Constitution. This objection is considered by Madison in Nos. 47 and 48 of *The Federalist*. The way in which he meets it is to point out that Montesquieu viewed the constitution of England as "the mirror of political liberty"; therefore, "not to mistake his meaning in this case, let us recur to the source from which the maxim was drawn." In this way Madison is able to substitute for Montesquieu's wrong account of the English constitution a true account, and thus, by correcting the premises of the argument, he reaches a different conclusion. Madison showed that no separation of powers exists in the English constitution, and that "the executive magistrate forms an integral part of the legislative authority." Hence he argues that no more practical significance should be imputed to Montesquieu's doctrine than that all the powers should not be united in the same hands. In this way he emptied the doctrine of the significance which Montesquieu himself ascribed to it, and was thus able to avoid an objection which was, in fact, well founded. The Constitution of the United States does not conform to Montesquieu's doctrine, and consideration of the debates of the constitutional convention show that it was not meant to do so. It aimed at a reproduction of the English constitution so far as was possible in the circumstances, and the English constitution then as now is founded on the connection of the powers.[1]

But though the powers were not separated, neither were they adjusted, which likewise was the case with the Constitution of England at the time the American version of it was made. That was beyond the thought

[1] A lucid exposition of the English system, displaying this connection, is contained in a pamphlet on the Constitution by James Iredell of North Carolina, published in 1788. See P. L. Ford's "Pamphlets on the Constitution of the United States," p. 347.

of the age. The particular adjustment eventually reached in English politics was facilitated by the practice of choosing secretaries of state from the membership of Parliament, but this practice was long antagonized by reformers, and an express prohibition of it was introduced by Tory influence in the Act of June 12, 1701, to regulate the succession to the Crown. Before any succession took place, and hence before the stipulation became operative, the prohibition was repealed by the Act of 1705, settling the matter by excluding from Parliament specified classes of office-holders, and by providing that a member who should accept office under the Crown must be reëlected by a constituency in order to retain his seat in the House of Commons. This established the English practice, which has remained substantially unchanged since then. The complete prohibition persistently sought for by eighteenth-century reformers, but frustrated in England, was however adopted in the Constitution of the United States.[1] This precludes such an adjustment as was reached in English politics — namely, the formation of the administration in the representative assembly itself. The way is, however, open to effect a connection of the powers by arrangements for the junction of the separately constituted executive and legislative departments. The practical expediency of this method is

[1] It is contained in Section 6 of Article 1, as follows: "No person holding any office under the United States shall be a member of either house during his continuance in office." The corresponding article in the Act of Settlement of 1701 provides that "no person who has an office or place of profit under the King, or receives a pension from the Crown, shall be capable of serving as a member of the House of Commons."

illustrated by the experience of Switzerland. In fundamental characteristics the American Constitution conforms to the Swiss type and is unconformable to the English type. Under the English system the Crown is a branch of the legislature; both in the American and in the Swiss system all legislative authority is vested in Congress. Under the English system executive authority is vested in a committee of the legislature; both in the American and in the Swiss system executive authority is vested in a distinct department of the government. The chief difference between the American system and the Swiss system is that the latter provides for systematic connection between the executive and legislative powers, while the former still lacks such connection.

From the first, American politics have been engaged in experimentation in this field. That there would be a connection was expected as a matter of practice and convenience, but as there is no express provision for it, the relations of the executive and legislative branches are exposed to disturbance from party violence and private interest. In this field the doctrine of the separation of the powers is still influential. It colors political ideas, supplies pretexts for discord, and obscures recognition of constitutional propriety. Our political history exhibits a series of precarious adjustments, but settled and obvious connection is yet to be accomplished, and it does not yet appear in what way it shall be. Still, we are able to note with certainty phases in the evolution of the American system, although we are not able to descry the form to which this evolution is tending. Political practice began with English procedure.[1] Congress relied upon the administration to prepare business for its consideration. So long as the connection of the powers of government lasted, the House of Representatives was the chief seat of dignity and power. On January 4, 1859, on the occasion of the removal of the Senate from the chamber it had occupied since 1819 to the chamber it now occupies, Vice-President Breckinridge delivered an elaborate historical address, in which he said: —

> "It would be interesting to note the gradual changes which have occurred in the practical working of the government since the adoption of the Constitution, and it may be appropriate to this occasion to remark one of the most striking of them: At the origin of the government, the Senate seemed to be regarded chiefly as an executive council. The President often visited the Chamber and conferred personally with this body; most of the business was transacted with closed doors, and it took comparatively little part in the legislative debates. The rising and vigorous intellects of the country sought the arena of the House of Representatives as the appropriate theater for the display of their powers. Mr. Madison observed, on one occasion, that being a young man, and desiring to increase his reputation, he could not afford to enter the Senate. . . ."

Similar testimony as to the original importance of the House is given by other experienced statesmen. Calhoun remarks that the House was originally "a much more influential body than the Senate." [2] Ben-

[1] When Jefferson was elected Vice-President in 1796, he prepared a manual of parliamentary law for his use as presiding officer of the Senate. It is a compilation of English parliamentary rules and precedents, and the preface mentions English procedure as "the model."

[2] Calhoun's Works, Vol. I, p. 341.

ton says, "For the first thirty years it was the controlling branch of the government, and the one on whose action the public eye was fixed." [1]

The cause of the decline of the House stands out plainly in our political history. The efficiency of the House is strictly proportioned to the connection between its legislative power and the executive power. The decline began as soon as the House began to reject executive aid and turned to committees of its own for the formulation of measures for its consideration. In 1797, Fisher Ames, a member of the House, in a letter to Alexander Hamilton, said: "Committees are already the ministers; and while the House indulges a jealousy of encroachment in its functions, which are properly deliberative, it does not perceive that these are impaired and nullified by the monopoly as well as the perversion of information by the committees." [2] The decline was arrested when the election of Jefferson brought the House and the administration into accord, and under him and his party successors the House attained its highest dignity and power. The change which settled the relations of the two houses to the advantage of the Senate took place during the administration of John Quincy Adams. The House and the administration were again antagonistic, and the connection of the powers was ruptured. Senator Benton, who was himself a congressional leader, observed this effect. He remarks: "The appointment of the majority of members in all committees, and their chairmen, in both houses, adverse to the administration,

[1] "Thirty Years' View," Vol. I, p. 208.
[2] Hamilton's Works, Vol. VI, p. 201.

was a regular consequence of the inflamed state of parties, although the proper conducting of the public business would demand for the administration the chairmen of several important committees as enabling it to place its measures fairly before the House." [1]

The breakdown of the Jeffersonian system of connection, through executive control of committee appointments, was the last of the adjustments aiming at direct connection between the administration and the House of Representatives. Thereafter adjustment of the powers of government was sought through extra-constitutional agencies of government — particularly in the development of the convention system, which first took definite shape in 1831. In theory the convention system proposes a system of representation combined with control of executive policy, and hence the great importance once attached to "platforms." In practice that system has displayed signal incompetency for the discharge of such functions, and it is now showing marked signs of decay. Conventions have no power to contract binding engagements. Their declarations are merely expressions of sentiment made for electioneering use, and those raised to office may decide for themselves to what extent and in what way they will recognize party obligations. Indeed explicit party pledges may be flatly repudiated. In 1896 the Republican party made an explicit pledge that if returned to power it would promote reciprocity agreements with foreign countries. The Dingley Tariff bill, passed by the Republican majority returned by the election of 1896, made special provision for the

[1] "Thirty Years' View," Vol. I, p. 92.

negotiation of reciprocity agreements, and the fact has been divulged that in making up the bill the committee fixed what it deemed to be an adequate rate for the protection of home industry, and then clapped on an additional rate for use as a concession in making reciprocity negotiations. But after a number of countries had responded to the invitation of the President extended in pursuance of the Dingley Act, and had entered into reciprocity agreements with this country, the Republican majority in the Senate refused to do so much as consider them. They expired in committee rooms, and the net result of the movement was simply an increase of the rates of duty above the scale actually intended in the passage of the act.

Quite as direct a repudiation of party pledges was made by Democratic members of Congress during the consideration of the Payne Tariff bill in 1909. The Democratic national platform of 1908 demanded "the immediate repeal of the tariff on wood-pulp, print paper, lumber, timber and logs, and that these articles be placed upon the free list." When the bill was under discussion in the House, over thirty Democrats voted against an amendment to make lumber free, and one of them was the chairman of the national convention which declared for free lumber. Later on seventeen Democratic senators voted in the same way, under the lead of Senator Bailey, who, when confronted by his party pledge, repudiated it, saying, "I refuse to allow a set of delegates, selected by the people absolutely without reference to a question of that kind, but selected almost solely with a view to the candidacies of men, to assemble in a convention and assume the function of legislators."[1] The criticism is well founded. The only pledges as regards public policy that are worth anything are such as are given by those who will have charge of public policy if elected, and are thus subjected to the steadying pressure of responsibility. Instructions from such irresponsible gatherings as nominating conventions are not entitled to binding force. But with the decay of the convention system, and the collapse of authority in its declarations of public policy, what connection is now left between elections and public policy? Really, none at all, save as the President is able to influence congressional action by diplomatic methods. He has no direct connection with Congress, but he must negotiate with members individually. He has not to deal with a legislature, but with numerous legislative segments. There are 72 committees of the Senate and 62 committees of the House. In the ordinary transaction of business nothing can be taken up for consideration except by permission of the committee to which the matter has been referred. Interests controlling committees are in a position to subordinate public policy to private interests.

The late Speaker Reed once summed up the situation as follows: —

"It is true we have at present irresponsible government, so divided that nobody can tell who is to blame. . . . Government by committees and of two houses entirely independent of each other produces some fearful and wonderful results. The growth of the British system was out of circumstances at least as bad as ours, and we shall find some way to responsible government, though it does not seem to me it will be the English way."[2]

[1] Congressional Record, Vol. 44, Part 3, May 24, 1909, p. 2333.

[2] Article published in *Illustrated American*, July 31, 1897, quoted in Bradford's "Lesson of Popular Government," Vol. II, p. 362 *et seq.*

The breakdown of representative government in the United States and the substitution of methods which give the custody of political power to particular interests, are the direct and natural consequence of the application of the doctrine of the separation of the powers. Viewing the situation from the standpoint of political pathology, it may be concisely described as a case of constitutional disease from specific infection. The case is a perfectly typical one, for which many parallels are to be found in history, the only marked difference being the remarkable vitality and endurance of the patient. In all other national constitutions which have experienced that infection, the breakdown was so rapid that all semblance of constitutional government rapidly disappeared. In France the outcome was a succession of constitutions, and there was no return of stability until the poison was expelled from the constitutional system.[1] The extrication of the states of Spanish America from a state of chronic revolution is attended by the substitution of connection for separation in the organization of public authority. History affords no instance of economical and efficient government constituted on the principle of the separation of the powers. On the other hand, it appears that where the rule of the people is most vigorous

[1] Compare the constitution of 1791 and the present one, adopted in 1875. The text will be found in Anderson's "Constitutions and Documents of France, 1789–1907." The constitution of 1791 denied the executive all legislative initiative. He "can only invite the legislative body to take the matter under consideration" (p. 77). The constitution of 1875 declares, "The President of the Republic has the initiative of the laws, concurrently with the members of the two Chambers" (p. 635).

there the connection is closest. The maximum of intimacy is presented in Switzerland, where the executive department frames all the laws and is in the habit of publishing for public information drafts of enactments in advance of their submission to the legislature for examination and action. The custody of the measures remains in the hands of the executive department during legislative consideration, and it drafts whatever changes are required as the result of discussion and criticism. The extraordinary economy of administration attained in Switzerland is striking evidence of the efficiency of the representative system when confined to its proper function as an organ of control in behalf of the people.

It has been noted that this doctrine of the separation of the powers, although it has profoundly affected procedure, was not adopted in the formation of the Constitution of the United States. It has produced its characteristic maladies by contaminating procedure under the Constitution and not by inoculating the Constitution itself. It is exhausting its influence in hindering adjustments necessary for administrative efficiency, but it is not destroying the powers of constitutional government; so means of control have been preserved which may be utilized as the stress of exigency compels improvement in the mechanism of government.

VII

POLITICAL CONDITIONS AND TENDENCIES

In the present lecture I shall endeavor to trace some of the consequences of the system of government described in the previous lecture, as bearing on the general subject of the cost of government. The examination will be necessarily incomplete, as the consequences are too voluminous to be reviewed within the bounds of any lecture, or indeed any one treatise; moreover, they permeate every part of the government, extending far beyond our immediate theme. One of the most baleful consequences is the decay of public justice, but that does not fall within the scope of these lectures. The consequences that we shall consider are exhibited both in state and federal government. The reactions of state politics upon the national finances are too important to be ignored.

In one respect, constitutional disease in state government has been advantageous to the development of national sovereignty. At the time the national government was founded its vital prospects were very dubious. Such a sober and circumspect judge of affairs as Benjamin Franklin, while anxious to give the republican form a trial, admitted that he did not have much hope of success, but thought that sooner or later the country would have to resort to kingship.[1]

[1] Madison's Journal, June 2, 4, and July 24, 1787.

At the outset the federal government was feeble as compared with the state governments. Vice-President Breckinridge, in the address referred to in the previous lecture, gave a striking account of the difficulties experienced in providing accommodations for the Federal government after the site had been selected. He says: —

> "Congress, either from indifference or the want of money, failed to make adequate appropriations for the erection of public buildings, and the commissioners were often reduced to great straits to maintain the progress of the work. Finding it impossible to borrow money in Europe, or obtain it from Congress, Washington, in December, 1796, made a personal appeal to the legislature of Maryland, which was responded to by an advance of $100,000; but in so deplorable a condition was the credit of the federal government that the state required, as a guarantee of payment, the pledge of the private credit of the commissioners."

Vice-President Breckinridge related that after the public buildings were burned by a British army on August 24, 1814, the federal government was again dependent upon charity. Congress met in a brick building known as Blodget's Hotel: —

> "But the accommodations in that house being insufficient, a number of public-spirited citizens erected a more commodious building on Capitol Hill, and tendered it to Congress; the offer was accepted, and both houses continued to occupy it until the wings of the new capitol were completed."

The general adoption of the principle of the separation of the powers in the framework of state constitutions soon began the destruction of representative government which is now so marked and which is still rapidly progressing. The separation between the executive and legislative departments perverted the functions of both so as to make them both odious, and it became the aim of the people to strip each of power so far as possible. Executive authority was disintegrated, and legislative authority was curtailed. A system of particular agency was gradually substituted for representative government, and representative assemblies, debarred from their proper function of control, came to be regarded as nuisances to be abated so far as possible. The perversion of constitutional government that has resulted is curiously illustrated by the written constitution of the very state that was in a position to patronize the federal government when that was just starting out. The constitution of Maryland declares that "the legislature ought to be frequently convened," which is a sound constitutional principle. Then it goes on to provide that the legislature shall not meet oftener than once in two years, and shall not continue in session longer than ninety days. Such manifest constitutional absurdity is common in American state constitutions. The fact is conclusive evidence of constitutional degeneracy, for if the representative assembly did in fact represent the people, to deny it facilities of meeting would deny the people the right to supervise and control the operations of the government. But in the absence of direct connection between the executive and the legislature, representative government is impossible, and only the name remains without the essence. Where systematic connection exists — as, for instance, in Switzerland — legislatures meet frequently, with the approval and esteem of the people. The Swiss federal congress meets regularly twice a year, and usually holds an extra session. But it meets only to consider measures submitted by the administration, and its sessions rarely last more than a few weeks.

Being debarred from efficient and economical government in the states from lack of its essential conditions, the people endeavored to get along with as little government as possible. Popular contempt and distrust of authority are deeply graven upon our existing state constitutions, as well as habitually expressed in the attitude of public opinion. This has had a vast influence in clearing the way for the development of national authority. In the national government executive authority is protected from disintegration. "The executive power shall be vested in a President." All executive agency exists by delegation of his authority subject to recall by his authority. Thus, however complex federal administration may become, it possesses the fundamental unity characteristic of sovereignty.

In the federal government sovereignty has remained intact, although embarrassed in its operations; in the states it has been dissipated. So, as an institutional fact, the sovereignty of the nation has no rivals within its bounds, and the expansion of its functions from weak and precarious beginnings has gone on with a rapidity unprecedented in history. When one considers the centuries of struggle and bloodshed that had to be passed through in accomplishing German national unity, one may form some idea of the important effect of state constitutional decay in promoting the growth of American national unity. If the field had been parcelled among systems of public authority as strong and as well organized as the states of Germany, the development of national unity would have been a far more difficult process. Since nation-making is the greatest political achievement which any people can perform, constitutional disease in America has entailed some indirect benefits. But these have all been secured, and now the atrophy of local function has pernicious reactions upon the federal government.

Traditional use of terms continues long after their vital content has disappeared, and so we still speak of state sovereignty just as at the time the federal Constitution was framed people still talked of the Holy Roman Empire, as if it were an actuality instead of a mere legal phrase.[1] The absurdity of the term "state sovereignty" could not have been more effectually demonstrated than by the proceedings of the federal courts during the extraordinary prevalence of railway enactments by state legislatures, occurring in close sequence to the cessation of supplies of railroad passes to state politicians. Offending states were arrested and taken to court almost as promptly as in police action with an ordinary drunk and disorderly case. At present state sovereignty is a sham, with no more solid content than a dead tree eaten out by white ants so that only the form remains.[2] The actual fact

[1] It did not become legally extinct until 1806, although moribund for centuries before.

[2] The juristic aspect of the process is considered by Professor W. W. Willoughby in "The American Constitutional System." He concludes that "looking at the matter from a purely legal standpoint, the individual commonwealths constitute simply governmental or administrative districts of the United States," p. 111.

It is sometimes assumed that extension of the jurisdiction of the courts in the field of public policy is a necessary incident of federal

is that state agency cannot be depended upon for public service, and this necessitates a federal duplication of administrative agency adding to the cost of government. No matter how great a transfer of function from state to federal authority takes place, state office-holders multiply to the extent of party ability to provide places for them, while the expansion of federal function involves a rapid increase of the federal pay-roll. In this respect the situation is peculiar. In other federal governments — for instance, Germany and Switzerland — transfer of function from state to federal authority means no more than a change in the site of the authority. The same functionaries who acted under state authority continue to act under federal authority.[1] Hence nothing more than a question of administrative expediency is involved when it is proposed to federalize any service, and in Switzerland the proposal is apt to come from the states themselves, to avoid boundary embarrassments among themselves. In this way, the control of dikes and forests has been put upon federal authority, and at

government. The experience of Germany and Switzerland shows that this is not so. Some indications of tendency in that direction in Germany were soon repressed. (See Lowell, "Government and Parties in Continental Europe," Vol. I, p. 282, etc.) The true cause of the force of that tendency in the United States is the misrepresentative character of the state governments. The courts are exercising the proper function of legislative assemblies, and, as usually happens in the development of vicarious function, it is poorly performed and is accompanied by dangerous stresses.

[1] According to the statement made in No. 36 of *The Federalist*, it seems that it was expected that a similar use of state agency might be made by the United States. But no tendency of the kind has been manifested in the practice of the federal government.

present the tendency is to centralize similarly the control and development of water-power. In Australia and Canada there is a similar disposition to treat all such questions from the standpoint of administrative economy and convenience, which indeed is the sensible way to look at them. Government exists for the public welfare and should be disposed with regard to the public welfare.

Circumstances have aroused the people to the fact that trying to get along with as little government as possible means defect in means of protecting public interests. In the states, actual sovereignty has passed largely from public trusteeship to private ownership. The corporation is stronger than the state. To use one of Burke's thrilling phrases, "it is not from impotence that we are to expect the tasks of power." People instinctively turn to the federal government for relief, and the federal government is responding. But, because of the circumstances that have been noted, this expansion of federal function involves far more than assumption of jurisdiction. It means the substitution of federal government for state government, resembling the process, in inverse order, by which national government was substituted for imperial government in Europe during the Middle Ages. Instead of involving merely adjustments of federal and state jurisdiction as in other existing systems of federal government, the process is moving towards an ouster of state authority from the field of government. If duplication of function goes on, if administrative responsibilities of state functionaries are taken over by federal authority leaving them in the position of useless drones, only the cost of state government will be left without corresponding benefit, and eventually the people will obtain relief from that burden. While no term may be set for the duration of the process, history warrants the conclusion that such must be the result, unless the process now going on be arrested.

The constitutional aspects of the situation are so profoundly important that I could not omit noting them, although it does not come within the scope of these lectures to pursue the subject any farther in this direction. I shall now proceed to make some categorical mention of present tendencies as regards the national finances.

1. *Increase in the Number of Federal Office-Holders*

It appears from statements compiled under the direction of the appropriation committees, in the first session of the 60th Congress, that the number of new offices created in excess of those abolished aggregated 10,682 (16,824 new, 6142 abolished), with salaries aggregating $9,087,987.50. During the same session the compensation attaching to 129,928 offices was increased by an aggregate of $9,146,575.20. Reductions of compensation were made in the case of two offices, the aggregate being $420. Thus in a single session the increase of government expenditure on account of salaries aggregated $18,234,142.70.[1]

The Official Register for 1909 (commonly known as the Blue Book) contains a list of federal office-holders,

[1] Senate Document No. 536, 60th Congress, 1st Session, pp. 616, 635.

aggregating 370,065. In 1816 the number was 6327; in 1863, 49,212. From 1871 to 1881 the number increased from 53,917 to 107,095. In 1899 the number was 208,215; so in the decade to 1909, the number was increased by 161,850, or over 16,000 a year.

This increase is the subject of party recrimination, but it is safe to say that it will continue. The opposition offers no remedy but that of reducing the exercise of governmental function, and that the people will not tolerate. The source lies beyond the reach of party action in Congress so long as conditions are as they are. The true nature of the case was exactly stated by Elihu Root in an address delivered at the dinner of the Pennsylvania Society in New York, December 12, 1906. He remarked: —

"The intervention of the National Government in many of the matters which it has recently undertaken would have been wholly unnecessary if the States themselves had been alive to their duty toward the general body of the country. It is useless for the advocates of State rights to inveigh against the supremacy of the constitutional laws of the United States or against the extension of National authority in the fields of necessary control where the States themselves fail in the performance of their duty. The instinct for self-government among the people of the United States is too strong to permit them long to respect any one's right to exercise a power which he fails to exercise. The Governmental control which they deem just and necessary they will have. It may be that such control would better be exercised in particular instances by the governments of the States, but the people will have the control they need either from the States or from the National Government; and if the States fail to furnish it in due measure, sooner or later constructions of the Constitution will be found to vest the power where it will be exercised — in the National Government."

2. *Increased State Demands on the Federal Treasury*

This was the subject of a memorial address delivered by Chairman Tawney of the House Appropriations Committee at Gettysburg, May 30, 1907.[1] He observed: —

"When any State increases its appropriations for any purpose, every legislator knows that that means an increase in the direct tax upon the people. Moreover, he knows that the people know this and that they watch with zealous care the tax rate which they must pay in cash from their own pockets. The legislator is slow to expose himself needlessly to the criticism and disapprobation of his constituents. Therefore needed legislation is postponed because of the expense it involves, and the Federal Government is appealed to, whenever possible, through the President, through the people's Representatives in Congress, and through the various Departments and bureaus of the Government."

He remarked that twenty-five years ago much of this federal intervention would not have been tolerated by the states now applying for it. He gave the following instances of the results of state mendicancy: —

"The recent surrender by the Southern States of the exercise of the right reserved to them by the Constitution to maintain, control, and regulate local quarantine, primarily because of the expense incident to the maintenance of an efficient State quarantine; the practical surrender to the Federal Government recently made by the State of Maryland of sovereignty over her oyster beds, that the State might be relieved of the cost of an accurate and necessary survey; the Federal inspection of the products of private manufacturing establishments and the sanitary inspection and control of the establishments themselves; the Federal inquiry into the physical, mental, and social conditions surrounding woman and child labor in all local industrial occupations, with a view

[1] Reprinted in the Congressional Record, 60th Congress, 1st Session, Vol. 42, No. 126.

ultimately to securing national legislation to regulate domestic occupation; the inspection of cattle, of insects, and of all agricultural products; the investigation of soils, in which the Federal Government has no interest; the care and disposition of timber on State lands set aside by the States as forest reserves; the actual breeding of horses and cattle, primarily for the benefit of the few fancy stock raisers of the country; the making of topographic and geological surveys of States in which the Government does not own a foot of unoccupied mineral or agricultural land; the making of topographic surveys of cities and counties, primarily for the benefit of municipalities, private owners of waterworks, and interurban and other electric railways; the free testing of coal by the Federal Government for the benefit of private owners of coal mines to determine its quality in heat units and the best and most economical utilization of the by-products; the free testing of building materials for the benefit of private individuals, contractors, and consulting engineers; the work of gauging streams that are nonnavigable, in States where the Federal Government owns no land and therefore has no jurisdiction or control over the streams gauged, a work which, as testified to by the former Director of the Geological Survey, is performed for the benefit of municipalities and 'primarily for the benefit of prospective investors in waterpowers.' These and many other undertakings which belong exclusively to the States or private interests to do and to pay for, but which have been authorized by Congress and must be paid for from appropriations made from the Federal Treasury, exceed the legitimate functions of the Federal Government as conceived by the founders of our political institutions and as declared by them in the Constitution of the United States."

3. *Increased District Demands through Nomination Conditions*

The spread of the direct primary system, by which a man makes a canvass for his party nomination on the basis of individual claims, incites Congressmen to persistent activity in securing appropriations for their districts. Here is a verbatim copy of the announcement of a Wisconsin congressional candidate: —

"Was instrumental in forcing the Child Labor Bill while a member of the District of Columbia Committee.

"He prevented the tearing up of the side-track to the Navy Yard, which if taken up would have closed down the Navy Yard, throwing hundreds of men out of work, and the excuse could be used that there was no way to get the raw material to the Navy Yard, and all the work would then be turned over to the Steel Trust.

"Introduced 80-cent Gas Bill. Compromised 90-cent Gas Bill which passed the Committee, and which is now on the calendar ready for passage. The citizens now pay $1.25 per 1000 cubic feet.

"Introduced a resolution to investigate the Government Printer and printing office, where thousands of dollars were being wasted and which caused the President to suspend Mr. Stillings, who a couple of weeks thereafter resigned.

"Defeated Section 9 of the Panama Bill, which was a rider and a joker to dismantle the Navy Yard and all Government buildings of their light and power plants, and to make a contract with the Washington Electric Light Co. The difference in the price of what the government was making it and which they wished to pay private corporations would be about $2,000,000 per year. This bill we defeated in the House, but it was put back in the Senate, and with the assistance of Senator La Follette and Senator Clark of Wyoming, again defeated the bill in the Senate.

"Also fought hard to defeat Section 6 of the Panama Bill, which read, 'Reduce the wages of the men in Panama 25 %.'

"He fought with Cooper and Nelson all the way through Congress against Cannon gag rule.

"He passed nine special pension bills for worthy old soldiers, which is a record for a new member as the rule is generally four.

"He worked with Congressman Stafford and procured an appropriation of $50,000 for a new Custom House warehouse to be built on the east side.

"He worked with Congressman Stafford to secure the appropriation of $75,000 for a new lightship to be placed in Milwaukee bay.

"He straightened out the Kinnickinnic River appropriation so that the city could go ahead with the work, and he stood by the President in all matters." [1]

When it is considered that hundreds of members are impelled by such motives and are shaping their action accordingly, the consequences to the public treasury may be imagined. The public interest is habitually subordinated to the particular interests cultivated by the member. The system thus substitutes particular agency for public representation, and the arts of local popularity are those by which the general welfare is undermined. The case recalls Burke's remark on the jobbing member of Parliament in the eighteenth century: "He may, while he betrays every valuable interest of the kingdom, be a benefactor, a patron, a father, a guardian angel, to his borough." [2]

4. *Increased Personal Demands through Nomination Conditions*

An extensive field for the formation and sale of political power as a business pursuit has long existed because of the multiplicity of elective offices in the states. In such conditions party organization exists rather as a means of controlling nomination patronage than as an agency of opinion; and hence, although party organization cannot detach itself from opinion, it tends to confine opinion to traditional forms, and seeks to repress the development of new issues. Dis-

[1] Advertisement in the *Evening Wisconsin*, August 29, 1908.

[2] "Thoughts on the Present Discontents."

satisfaction with existing conditions, to find practical expression, must cope with enormous organization tasks in the formation of a new party, or must pierce the organization of existing parties, against the opposition of vested interests established in control of the organization. Efforts to establish new parties to secure practical consideration of new issues have been made successfully, and, indeed, all existing national parties are the outcome of such efforts, their claim of lineal descent from the party organizations of the first period of the Republic being more fictitious than real. But conditions have become so complex that it is now easier to break down the organization of an old party than to find the amount of capital and administrative ability required to establish a new one. With the enormous increase of the national wealth, and with the huge values created in all public utilities by the growth of population and trade, the mastery over the disposition of such resources that goes with party control has made the emoluments of professional politics more and more enviable and attractive. Competition is so brisk and so great an amount of skilled political talent is available for insurgent movements, that in every direction the old controls are breaking down, opening new fields for political adventure. It is a process similar to that which went on in the Roman Republic when politics broke the bounds of patrician dictation and political power was opened to any one who could ingratiate himself with the masses. The outcome varied all the way from a Cicero to a Cataline, but from the economic standpoint the process meant that the public estate was drawn upon to meet the costs of the electoral process. As in the end there is but one fund from which all costs of government — direct or indirect — must be defrayed, namely, the national wealth; it follows that the greater the cost of elections becomes, the greater becomes the cost of government, and that as elections are multiplied waste of resources is increased. Where the direct primary has been substituted for the convention system it has enlarged the arena in which political power may be sought and captured, but it has greatly increased the cost. The electioneering organization which the old convention system supplied to the protégés of the party managers must now be sought and paid for by individual candidates.[1] The result is not only a heavy general increase in the cost of officering the public service in state government, but also in carrying on congressional elections. Since 1897 Wisconsin has had a law compelling the filing of statements of electioneering expenses. In 1904 the direct primary was made compulsory. It appears that the acknowledged cost of candidacy for the House of Representatives has increased from $19,437.75 in 1898 to $50,417.79 in 1908. The cost of candidacy to the United States Senate was returned in 1905 as being $262.87 ; in 1907, $6187.89 ; in 1909, $192,977.59.[2]

[1] It should be remembered that when representative government is founded consistently with its essential characteristic, elections are held only for the selection of the representatives of the people. Therefore candidacy is always local, and no elaborate organization is required.

[2] Chapter XIX of "Political Reform in Wisconsin," a thoughtful treatise written and published by E. L. Philipp of Milwaukee, Wisconsin, contains an exhibit of electioneering expenses taken from

In such conditions it is a natural consequence that there should be a keen desire on the part of members of Congress to increase their pay and emoluments. It is an ordinary trait of human nature to magnify one's own value, and to regard one's pay as an inadequate recognition of it. Whenever opportunity exists to fix the rate of compensation for oneself by oneself, it is fixed higher than when others do the fixing. Legislators everywhere are apt to think themselves poorly requited for their labors, and the tendency to seek higher compensation is by no means confined to the American Congress. While gathering material for these lectures I came upon one issue of the *London Times* [1] which contained reports of three movements of the kind. In Italy a bill was proposed raising the pay of senators and deputies to $1200 a year; in Prussia, the lower house of the Diet passed a resolution in favor of the grant of free railway passes, in

the public records. In the city of Milwaukee the expenses of all city officers increased from $8280.93 in 1898 to $50,479.49 in 1908. The case of Mayor Rose is very striking. His popularity is attested by the fact that he was elected five out of six times when a candidate, but his expenses increased from $933.25 in 1898 to $5223.89 in 1908. He was defeated in 1906 when he spent $2027.10 by a candidate who spent $9207.91. It should be remembered that the expenses returned by a candidate are not necessarily all the expenses incurred by his candidacy. If his friends choose to spend money in his interest, that does not belong to the personal expenditure he is bound to state. The friendly concerts of action that obtain in high finance, and the business value of having a friend in power, might secure large expenditures without notice of it to the beneficiary so that he could make a low return with a clear conscience. When political conditions are such that power may be bought instead of earned, it certainly will be bought.

[1] Weekly edition, *London Times*, May 14, 1909.

addition to their pay of $3.75 a day during the session; and in the British House of Commons a resolution was passed by a vote of 242 against 92 in favor of the payment of members "and for the transfer to the imperial exchequer of the financial responsibility for returning officers' expenses." The resolution simply asserted the principle, but the salary mentioned in the discussion was $1500 a year. In these cases the allowance cannot be made unless recommended by the administration, which thus must assume the responsibility for it before the electorate, and if members should attempt to force the government they could not do so without being regarded by their constituencies as bolters, and hence they would forfeit their party standing. But in the case of the American Congress, no such responsibility exists. Members of all parties can work together to help themselves, and at the same time manage to avoid responsibility. The thing may be wrapped up in some essential bill and members in ticklish districts may be provided with specious pleas to the effect that they had to submit in order to save important legislation. It is a thing which is admitted by congressional politicians to require nice handling, since if any location of responsibility can be made by the voters, there may be an upsetting upheaval. But the matter has been so astutely managed that members have raised their pay to $7500 a year together with steadily increasing perquisites in the way of personal supplies and comforts, and of patronage in their individual award.[1] It is a curious circumstance that

[1] Among the perquisites of a member is the right to make free distribution of 20,000 packages of vegetable and 2000 packages of

the greatest development of luxury and opulence in any legislative assembly has been attained in the American Republic. The Capitol is a large building, but not large enough to supply the personal conveniences required by members, and two new large office buildings have been erected with rich appointments.[1]

flower seed. The agricultural department is expected to put them up and mail them, using bundles of addressed franks provided by the member for the purpose. The Postmaster-General reports that in 1909 the expense to the government for free mail under congressional frank was $515,385. (See Congressional Record for January 29, 1910, Vol. 45, No. 32, p. 1196, etc., for a discussion of the practice.) The *Nashville Banner* of January 20, 1910, published the following: —

"Congressman Korbly, of Indiana, who recently sent nearly a carload of bags of seed to his constituents through the mails on his congressional frank, admits that he abused the franking privilege and that he opposes the continuance of such abuses; but he says that as long as they continue he intends to see that his share of government seeds are distributed. This is equivalent to saying that although he condemns the wrong he proposes to continue to do the wrong as long as the opportunity is afforded and other members do it."

[1] During Senate debate on the legislative appropriation bill, March 24, 1910, a discussion arose over the employment of a professional masseur for the Senate at a yearly salary of $1800. In the course of it Senator Hale made the following statement in regard to the bath-rooms: —

"It is true enough what the Senator from Nebraska has said, that while bath-rooms are luxuries and not essential to the maintenance of official life during the hours of the day that we are here, we have always had them in the Senate; and when I was a Member of the House, they had been there for years in the House wing of the Capitol building; and, as the Senator may know, there are handsome marble bath-rooms which are used when a Member sees fit to use them.

"When these two new buildings were created that feature was adopted by the committee in charge and by the superintendent,

Positions connected with the up-keep and service of the legislative buildings and offices are in the direct bestowal of members of Congress, and are parceled among the members so that they can make individual awards.[1] To these privileges members of the minority

and we have come now to the point where it is put in black and white who they are, what they shall be paid, and how many there are of them.

"The bath-rooms are handsome, but they are not handsomer than those for the House of Representatives. They are marble; they are the best that can be made. Whether the man in charge should be a professional masseur is not a very important matter. It does not detract anything from him if he is a professional masseur, and if any Senator wants to be treated instead of being treated in his own house he can be treated there.

"The Committee on Rules and the superintendent in charge have presented to the Committee on Appropriations this list. The Senator from Nebraska is entirely right; almost all of this list — the stenographers, the messengers in charge — is essential. It is an immense building. Hundreds of people and thousands of people go there every day. There ought to be toilet rooms and closets and supervision, and all that. Those are essential. The bath-rooms are in, and whether you will have a man in charge, as I have said, who is a professional and an educated masseur is not a matter of great importance.

"I hope the Senator from Kansas, in accordance with the suggestion of the Senator from Nebraska, instead of striking out all of the provision, if he is especially interested in limiting and making simpler the bath-room part of it, will let us deal with that; but these other things have got to be done. You cannot have a building of that kind without them. It is a favorite building. Senators go there. Almost every Senator has rooms there, and you have got to keep it up. It costs money, and somebody has got to pay the bills." Congressional Record, Vol. 45, No. 78, p. 3792.

[1] Under the English system all these appointments are made by the administration through estimates submitted to Parliament for approval under rules of order which do not admit of motions for increase of the appropriations recommended.

are admitted. Some frugal members supplement their official income by appointing members of their own family to positions as clerk, messenger, or laborer. The direct connection between this patronage and the personal interests of the members is illustrated by the practice which exists of voting an extra month's pay to employees at the close of the session. Since Congress is in session only about seven months in long session years and only three months in alternate years, the service is not onerous, but extra compensation is regularly voted as a transfer to public account of liabilities that else might fall upon members individually. The following candid explanation of the practice was made by Mr. Keifer of Ohio when the matter came up at the close of the first session of the sixty-first Congress : —

"The theory of the rule for the payment of a month's extra pay to employees of the House is, that as they are usually brought here for the session from distant parts, from the districts in the different States as a fair mode of distribution of the patronage, that they should be paid something on account of extra expenses. They come here now as they did long ago, and we pay them now not as much in proportion to increased cost of living as they were paid long ago. We pay them for the session only, and generally with the greatest economy they spend that salary during the session. They draw no mileage and nothing for expenses, and this rule grew up out of the idea that at the end of a session they ought to have an extra month's pay to enable them to go home. I have heard it said on the floor long ago in a Democratic House, that it was better perhaps to appropriate this extra month's pay than for the Members to contribute to pay their expenses home [*laughter*], and I think the rule grew up out of such a matter as that." [1]

[1] Congressional Record, August 4, 1909, p. 5141.

The spirit in which members use their opportunities is illustrated by the following extract from House debate relative to a legislative commission that visited Europe to investigate immigration: —

"Mr. MACON. I am advised, so far as that is concerned, that the gentleman from New York [Mr. BENNET] appointed several persons connected with this immigration investigation who are constituents and friends of his. I do not know whether that is true or not.

Mr. BENNET of New York. That is true. I appointed all I could get.

Mr. MACON. And at as high salaries as you could get for them and as many as you could get?

Mr. BENNET of New York. That I admit, and so did every member of the commission."

* * * * * * *

"Mr. MACON. I said I had heard the gentleman did make appointments of many of his friends.

Mr. BENNET of New York. I will say to the gentleman from Arkansas that I did appoint every one that I could, wherever I found a competent man to do the work, and I got every appointment I could, the same as we did for every Member of the House that came to us — Democrats or Republicans."[1]

As a result of such tendencies the expenditure on legislative account is enormously greater than in other countries. The British Estimates for 1907 provide a gross allowance of £42,543 (about $212,000) for the House of Lords; and £60,250 (about $300,000) for the House of Commons.[2] These amounts cover the cost of the official staff of the houses of Parliament. For

[1] Congressional Record, January 25, 1910, Vol. 45, No. 28, p. 981. It appeared in the course of debate (p. 945) that the commission had expended $657,992.67, and wanted more.

[2] House of Commons Sessional Papers, 51, 1907, pp. 77, 83.

maintenance of buildings, furniture, fuel, stationery, printing, and general supplies, there are additional estimates aggregating £196,170 (about $980,000) — a total of $1,492,000, against which there is a set-off amounting to £32,450 (about $162,000) for fees, as under the rules certain charges are made for committee hearings on private bills. Thus the net charge upon the public treasury for the Parliament of the United Kingdom was $1,330,000 as against $13,788,886 in 1908 for the Congress of the United States.[1] The House of Lords is composed of 615 members, our Senate of 92; the House of Commons is composed of 670 members, our House of Representatives of 391 members.

The public printing is a bottomless sink-hole in our finances. The entire amount appropriated in 1908 by the British Parliament was £748,053 (about $3,740,000), "to defray the expenses of providing stationery, printing, paper, binding, and printed books for the public service; to pay the salaries and expenses of the stationery office; and for sundry miscellaneous services, including reports of parliamentary debates." It is simply impossible to get at the corresponding expenditure in the federal government, as the departments purchase their own supplies. Congressional expenditure in 1908 included $6,394,810 for the "Public

[1] Report of the Secretary of the Treasury for 1909, p. 21. There are heavy items of legislative department expenditure, covered by appropriations for executive department expenditure. For instance, the cost of congressional seed supplies is put upon the agricultural department, and the cost of congressional mail matter is put upon the post-office department. An accurate classification of expenditure, such as is made by the British Estimates, would make the comparison still more discreditable to our national legislature.

Printer." In this one item alone many millions of dollars can be saved annually by consolidation of service and ordinary precautions against waste.[1]

5. *Increased Hostility to Executive Authority*

The sort of management which Congress now applies to matters within its own exclusive province it continually seeks to extend to the other departments of the government. In discussing the legislative department Madison remarked: "It is against the enterprising

[1] Senator Carter in the course of debate said: —

"Infinite duplication occurs in the various departments of the Government. We have eight or ten different map-making departments now working in the city of Washington, some making maps for the Coast and Geodetic Survey, others making maps for the War Department, others making maps for the Post-Office Department, others making maps for the Interior Department, and so on down the line. One map-making concern, with a number of skilled men, could perform all of the work with a moiety of the cost. So it is with printing. Every department of the Government proceeds in its own way with the printing of documents, and this abuse has continued until we are now renting extra buildings in the city of Washington to house the great accumulation of useless documents duplicated indefinitely." Congressional Record, February 21, 1910, Vol. 45, No. 50, p. 2205.

The following statement occurs in a committee report submitted to the House of Representatives: —

"The entire number of old pamphlets and publications which are now in the folding room and for which there is practically no demand exceeds a million copies. There is in the vaults perhaps a thousand tons of worthless printed paper, which cumbers the earth and is of no value to any one. The great volume of such a mass of publications, for which there is no demand and of which the folding room is making practically no distribution, shows, it seems to the committee, the necessity for some action on the part of the House." Congressional Record, January 8, 1910, Vol. 45, No. 15, p. 436.

ambition of this department that the people ought to indulge all their jealousy and exhaust all their precautions." Congress holds a contrary opinion, and its favorite attitude is that of vigilant concern lest the enterprising ambition of the executive department shall overthrow the republic and set up royal state on its ruins. When the appropriations for the executive department are under consideration, congressional oratory resounds in favor of economy. But in 1908, when the disbursements for the legislative department aggregated $13,788,886.42, those for the executive department aggregated $404,523.50.[1] In this respect the cost of American government stands in shining contrast to that of other countries, in which — with the exception of Switzerland — the cost of maintaining the offices of the chief magistrate far exceeds that borne by the United States. It is in the field of congressional cost that the comparison is humiliating and disgraceful to the American people.

While Congress is fond of viewing with alarm the increase in the cost of government, it keeps augmenting it by continual effort to extend congressional patronage by means of stipulations annexed to the appropriations, and any attempt at executive economy meets with inflexible opposition. During President Roosevelt's administration an executive commission, commonly known as the Keep Commission, was appointed to study departmental methods. That commission made a report recommending changes that would reduce the cost and increase the efficiency of the public service. Congress paid no attention to the report, but a proviso known

[1] Report of the Secretary of the Treasury for 1909, p. 21.

as the Tawney amendment was included in the Sundry Civil Appropriation bill of the session, prohibiting any further action of the kind by the executive department.[1] Congress itself is always willing to appoint committees or commissions from its own membership, and to repeat the process as often as an occasion presents itself. Every new creation of the sort provides a fresh batch of offices to be filled.[2]

[1] It is as follows: —

"That hereafter no part of the public moneys, or of any appropriation heretofore or hereafter made by Congress, shall be used for the payment of compensation or expenses of any commission, council, board, or other similar body, or any members thereof, or for expenses in connection with any work or the results of any work or action of any commission, council, board, or other similar body, unless the creation of the same shall be or shall have been authorized by law, nor shall there be employed by detail, hereafter or heretofore made, or otherwise, personal services from any executive department or other government establishment in connection with any such commission, council, board, or other similar body." (Acts of 1909.)

[2] During Senate debate on a proposal to appoint one of these commissions to investigate departmental methods, Mr. Dolliver remarked: —

"We have had these business methods examined by joint commissions and special commissions and by special committees of both Houses of Congress within the last few years. The Dockery Commission spent months of time in the exact kind of research that is proposed here. More recently committees of the House on the expenditures in the various departments spent a good deal of time upon the same subject. In the later months of the last administration, a committee of experts chosen from the departments, known informally in Congress as the 'Keep Commission,' went through all their business methods and made such suggestions as seemed to them to be reasonable and desirable; and only a short time ago a joint commission selected from the Post-Office Committees of the two Houses with the aid of high-priced experts, overhauled all the business methods of the Post-Office Department and made

Meanwhile the actual practice of Congress is to complicate still further the business methods of the departments and to swell the cost of government by manipulating appropriations in aid of patronage. How the thing goes on was thus explained in the course of House debate on an appropriation bill: —

"Mr. Gillett. In framing our bill we frequently have Members of Congress come to us and speak in favor of this and that clerk and ask for a promotion, and it is one of the most unpleasant features of this legislative bill, to avoid giving offense and at the same time not to create the impression which we all can see would be fatal in the departments, that the promotion of a clerk depends not on his efficiency, but having a friend in the House of Representatives.

I remember, in a conference not a great many years ago, when the Senate asked an increase of salary for a clerk in a certain division, we responded that we had already given the chief of that division everything that he had asked, whereupon a Senator said, 'I have a letter upon this subject,' and he innocently and carelessly read to us a letter which we found was addressed to another Senator from the head of this division, in which he said: —

'If you wish to accomplish the object you have in view and raise the salary of such a person, the way to do it is by the following language.'

It was obviously a mere attempt to accomplish the promotion of a personal friend. Such things have happened in the past, and such things are happening now, but in many departments the system of promotion by efficiency has been adopted, which to a certain extent remedies this, but the trouble is you cannot entirely remedy it until you have a system by which the compensation of the clerks and the promotion of the clerks depends upon the kind and character of work they do. That would change the whole atmosphere, and that could be accomplished by adopting the re-

such suggestions as they thought were wise and appropriate to a Congress which placidly ignored the whole subject." Congressional Record, February 21, 1910, Vol. 45, No. 50, p. 2202.

port of the Keep Commission, to which the gentleman a little while ago referred." [1]

Instances of the tendencies that have been noted might be multiplied. I have presented some characteristic specimens of congressional action, and there are many more to be found in the course of any congressional session if one has the patience to wade through the Record. There is abundant evidence to show that while Congress may favor economy in the abstract, it does not favor economy in practice, and that existing conditions of congressional action tend, either directly or indirectly, to swell the cost of government. Moreover, the present tendency is to break down what remains of executive authority in the management of the public business. The aim of Congress appears to be to supersede the President in the control and direction of the executive departments. For instance, if you examine the Miscellaneous Appropriations Act of May 30, 1908, you will notice that it issues instructions to the Secretary of War and the Secretary of the Treasury, directing them to do various things involving an expenditure of $33,368,500. It is put up to the President to say whether or not he will approve the bill, but when he does, the terms of the enactment seem to forbid him any right to interfere with the performance of the work. The legislative department, having lost its own proper constitutional function, is apparently on its way to destroy the proper function of the President. The situation presents issues involving the very existence of constitutional government.

[1] Congressional Record, March 21, 1910, Vol. 45, No. 75, p. 3533.

VIII

POSSIBILITIES OF IMPROVEMENT

After such an exhibition of governmental characteristics and tendencies as I have had to make in the previous lectures of this course, you may be apt to think that matters are going from bad to worse. It is quite probable that matters will be worse before they are better, but it would be a mistake to think that there are no signs of improvement. There are such signs, and it will be the purpose of this lecture to point them out.

Improvement may come either by congressional action or by executive action. After the criticism I have been compelled to make upon congressional methods, it is a pleasure to be able to say that great improvements have already been effected through congressional action. Bad as things are, they would be a great deal worse save for reforms which from time to time have been instituted by Congress. The public mind is now so sensitive on the subject that it is experiencing the usual illusion of regarding increased perception of evil as evidence of the growth of evil. It is true that present conditions tend to profuse expenditure, but it is also true that means of effective control are beginning to take shape. On taking a large view of things we can see that the federal government has been moving towards constitutional methods, slowly, heavily, and by clumsy lurches, rather than by steady progress, but, nevertheless, great progress has been made.

At the time the federal Constitution was adopted, budget control was nowhere established in an exact and definite form, although at that very time Pitt was introducing the system of unified control on which the present English system of budget control rests. Indeed, the Consolidated Fund, which is the basis of that system, was formed in 1786, the year before the meeting of the Constitutional Convention in Philadelphia. The ancient system was that the Crown carried on the government with the aid of grants and supplies furnished from time to time by the Commons, the Crown having full power of disposition over the revenue thus obtained. The influence of this tradition is seen in Jefferson's action as Secretary of State at the outset of Washington's administration. He visited the Senate chamber to advise the Senate to make a lump appropriation for the diplomatic service to be apportioned according to the discretion of the President.[1]

The language of the Constitution of the United States on this point reflects the vagueness of the English system prior to the reforms introduced by Pitt. All it has to say is that "no money shall be drawn from the treasury, but in consequence of appropriations made by law; and a regular statement and account of the receipts and expenditures of all public money shall be published from time to time." [2] This

[1] Maclay's Journal, p. 272.

[2] Art. 1, Sec. 9. The instruction of example and experience not open to the statesmen of 1787 is visible in the action taken

provision was not held to compel annual reports until the year 1800. Important advances toward budget control were made by the acts of July 12, 1870, and June 20, 1874. These measures, due chiefly to the advocacy of Mr. Dawes and Mr. Garfield while members of the House, required all unused appropriations to be covered into the Treasury. Enormous sums had been accumulated by the departments as unexpended balances. The amounts returned to the Treasury under these acts aggregated $174,000,000. In a single bureau there was an unexpended balance of $36,000,000, the accumulation of a quarter of a century.[1] What could more pointedly display the futility of congressional control over appropriations by committees acting upon private representations made by bureau chiefs! Treasury disbursements are still, however, far from being subject to systematic control through annual appropriations as in England. There is a class of continuing appropriations, expenditures from which are not confined to fiscal years. From a return made by the Secretary of the Treasury in 1908, it appears that disbursements aggregating $118,865,898 were made in 1907 by virtue of a continuing authority in the management of various special funds.[2]

by the framers of the Confederate Constitution, March 11, 1861. In it Art. 1, Sec. 9, contained the following clause: —

"Congress is forbidden to appropriate money from the treasury except by a vote of two thirds of both houses, unless it be asked by the head of a department and submitted by the President, or be asked for the payment of its own expenses, or of claims against the Confederacy declared by a judicial tribunal to be just."

[1] These facts are given in an instructive address by Mr. Theodore E. Burton of Ohio, delivered in the House on March 15, 1904, on the general subject of budget control.

[2] House Document No. 871, 60th Congress, 1st Session.

The subject of economical reform is now engaging the attention of Congress. The action taken affords another illustration of the futility of the committee system of control. The Senate, among its 72 standing committees, has eight charged with the examination of departmental expenditures. But when the piling up of Treasury deficits in 1909 excited alarm, the Senate deemed it necessary to create still another committee on the general subject of public expenditures. It is the largest of the committees, having twenty members, including the chairmen of the committees on Appropriations, Finance, Military Affairs, Naval Affairs, Post-Offices, Agriculture, and Indian Affairs. So it brings together the heads of the principal spending committees with a view of coördinating their action, a purpose not logically reconcilable with the individual license of action possessed by senators. This committee was appointed on March 22, 1909. After some months it made a report, reiterating what had often been said before, and is perfectly well known; namely, that "the application to the business of the government of improvements in system and method similar to those which have produced the high degree of business efficiency in the great business corporations of the country will result in the saving of many millions of dollars annually and in a much higher degree of efficiency in the conduct of the government business." The committee recommended a business methods commission composed of three senators, three representatives, and three members selected by the President. On February 5, 1910, Senator Aldrich introduced a bill for the creation of such a commission. In advocating the bill Senator Aldrich made some very frank admissions. He declared that a saving of over $100,000,000 a year could be readily effected, and later on he declared: "If I were a business man and could be permitted to do it, I would undertake to run this government for $300,000,000 a year less than it is now run for." [1]

Congressional jealousy of the executive department promptly manifested itself. Mr. Money, the opposition party leader, protested against any association of the executive and legislative branches of the government. His remarks struck a responsive chord. Senator Aldrich held that "as it is an investigation into the executive management, the executive departments should take part in it"; but a little later in the same day he proposed to strike out the provision in regard to appointees by the President "in deference to the expressed opinion of senators." On February 28, 1910, Senator Newlands proposed a substitute providing for a commission of nine to be appointed by the President, supporting it by a speech much sounder in constitutional doctrine than is usually heard in the Senate. But his efforts were fruitless. The substitute was rejected without a call for the ayes and nays. The bill as passed by the Senate merely provides for a joint commission of five members of the Senate and five members of the House. Try to fancy such a situation arising in the affairs of any private business corporation: the executive management denied any part in the ordering of its affairs!

[1] Congressional Record, February 21, 1910, Vol. 45, No. 50, pp. 2202–2203.

All that the movement amounts to is the creation of a new committee subject to the same conditions of action as the old committees, and there can be no sensible expectation of much better results. It should be observed that all the improvements in system that have been accomplished have been favored by the propensity of Congress to keep departmental officers in a state of dependence upon the congressional committees. It is quite another matter when reforms strike at congressional patronage. President Taft has himself pointed out in his public addresses that as soon as any change concerning the pay and quantity of offices is proposed those affected will appeal to their friends in Congress for help, which these friends in Congress are apt to extend.[1] The long-urged and continually defeated consolidation of pension agencies, to which I referred in a previous lecture, is a typical instance.

The truth of the matter is that Congress lacks power of self-amendment. It is the servant of particular interests, and its energies are consumed by that service. Such invariably is the case unless the organization of public authority sets up effective barriers against local demands and class importunity. Edmund Burke long ago laid down a principle of universal application when he said of the British Parliament, "If we do not permit our members to act upon a very

[1] In a speech at Newark, New Jersey, on February 23, 1910, President Taft said: —

"They will find opposition in Congress to every change recommended, because there is no branch or bureau so humble that it cannot secure its adherents and defenders within the legislative halls."

enlarged view of things, we shall infallibly degrade our national representation into a confused and scuffling bustle of local agency." That is the matter with our Congress. The cause was indicated by Mr. Burton of Ohio, in the speech in the House on March 15, 1904, to which I have already referred. He said: —

"The most characteristic feature can be expressed in one word — the word 'severance.' First, the severance of the executive department from the legislative; next, the severance of the committees or branches of the legislature which provide the revenue from those which determine expenditures; and third, the severance of the committees which consider estimates and present appropriation bills."

All these sorts of severance are parts of a series, the first of which, and the cause of all the rest, is the severance of the executive and legislative departments. Constitutional government, with its prime characteristic, — budget control, — is impossible without a connection of the powers.

Constitutional history often illustrates the truth of a remark made by the philosopher Schopenhauer to the effect that we fancy that important events will make their entrance on the stage of affairs with the noise of drums and trumpets, whereas they slip in unobtrusively and almost unnoticed. I well remember the surprise I felt when in the course of my reading I discovered that what our text-books now designate as the fall of the Roman Empire was unobserved by the people of that age. The epochal character of the event as set forth in history is apt to give one the notion of an appalling smash; but it appears that when the Roman Empire fell nobody heard it fall. The significance of the event was not appreciated until centuries afterwards. And in the same way the germs of all great institutional developments have emerged without manifesting their importance. The whole framework of modern government is traceable to usages of barbarians adopted from considerations of convenience and without any perception of constitutional values. It seems to me that Congress, by sheer stress of circumstances, has been forced to take a step towards connection of the powers and has thus unwittingly started a movement of profound constitutional importance. The real hope of establishing budget control, and with it a genuine constitutional system, lies in the flow of political force in the channel thus opened. I refer to section 7 of the Sundry Civil Appropriation Act of March 4, 1909, making it the duty of the President to coördinate income and expenditure.[1]

Most assuredly this law was not enacted with the view of enhancing presidential authority. Its author inserted in the same act a clause stripping the President of any authority to employ experts to institute reforms in departmental organization, such as President Roosevelt had endeavored to accomplish through the labors of the Keep Commission. Section 7 probably derives its origin from the same animus, for as has been mentioned previously it is a pet theory of the congressional leaders that the rapid increase of expenditure is largely due to popular demands incited by President Roosevelt's influence. But whatever be the motive, the action taken is the salvation of representative government in the United States.

[1] See Appendix B for the text of the provision.

This is a pretty broad statement to make, but it is abundantly warranted. What has been the cause of the wreckage of republics so thickly strewn over the records of the past? Simply this, that the people would much rather indulge the passions and appetites of one ruler than of many rulers. Time was, when the very name of republic became odious to the people, and prejudice against it colored popular literature. You will see this sticking out in Oliver Goldsmith's novel, the "Vicar of Wakefield," in which one of the characters mentions the republics of Holland, Genoa, and Venice as places in which "the laws govern the poor and the rich govern the laws." Something of the same kind is at times said of our own republic, and if the people continue to think that way and have reason for it, and if no other means of escape were possible, they would eventually do as all other peoples so circumstanced have done in the past, — resort to monarchical absolution. Whether the office be called King, or Protector, or President, is a minor consideration. The essence of the situation is that the mass of the people will not submit to be preyed upon under constitutional forms, and what they cannot mend they will end.

In these times when Darwinism is in the air, I shall not have to argue that the tendency heretofore of the monarchical type of government to survive and of the republican type to perish, implies on the whole superior fitness of the monarchical type in past periods. The science of politics is sufficiently well advanced to enable us to say in what that fitness consisted. If any one wants to check off my averments by reference to the authorities, I recommend Sidgwick's "Development of European Polity," and particularly Chapters 21 and 22 of that treatise. He brings out very plainly that monarchy waxed strong because it represented the principle of national unity, and it was able to do so because it substituted for the rule of many "the rule of that which is intrinsically and *per se* one." Thus Crown authority by its very nature subordinates the parts to the whole, by taking away from the parts any legal power of action. That is to say, it sacrifices liberty to order, on the principle stated by Madison "that the safety and happiness of society are the objects at which all political institutions aim, and to which all such institutions must be sacrificed."[1] The problem that must be solved to avert such sacrifice, and to assure the stability of republican government, is to subordinate the parts to the whole while allowing them powers of legal action. If that can be accomplished, the republic is incontestably the superior type, for it is energized in all its parts and is thus capable of the highest efficiency.

Just such an agency of national sovereignty has long been in process of formation, with the presidential office as its basis. We may even fix the exact time when the movement in this direction obtained constitutional definition. It was promulgated by President Polk in his message of December 5, 1848, in which he pointed out that "the President represents in the executive department the whole people of the United States, as each member of the legislative department represents portions of them." President Polk made

[1] *The Federalist*, No. 64.

this statement in defense of presidential activity in directing legislative action. But the function of general representation that has settled upon the presidential office as the only available basis for it, lacks appropriate institutions for its discharge. The people look to the President to do what he is denied means of doing. The dilemma that ensues was well stated by President Taft in his speech at Rochester on March 18, 1910. After giving a list of the measures he was urging upon the attention of Congress, he remarked: —

> "One great difficulty about being President, and I assure you there are a great many of them, is that he is the titular head of the party, and is made responsible for the laws adopted by the party, although he has had nothing more to do with them than a recommendation at the beginning and the power of veto at the end. He is held responsible for all of the promises made by the party. And if, in his enthusiasm and desire to fulfil the party pledges and to help the country, as he thinks, he goes about and consults all the interests so as to recommend a fair law and makes suggestions to Congress, and some Congressmen differ with him, he is held up as a tyrant trying to force his views down the throats of unwilling Congressmen and unwilling Senators.
>
> "And so he is in a bad fix. On the one hand it is said of him that he is not doing what he ought to do, and on the other hand he is trying to frighten an unwilling Congress to do what it doesn't want to do."

A good deal is being said about President Taft's loss of popularity. Well, that may be a transient phenomenon, and before he gets through things may be different. It would not be worth while mentioning, and would, indeed, be out of place here, were it not for the fact that popular resentment attaches to this very point of defect in his representative function.

For instance, I find in the *Newark Evening News*, an independent newspaper, the following: —

"Mr. Taft says himself that the President is the one representative of the entire people under our form of government. But he will not take a step for their interests without definite mandate by law. Is there some move Mr. Taft can make for the people? He does not ask, 'Is there any law that prohibits me from making this move?' He does ask, 'Is there any law that definitely orders me to make this move?' If there is not, he does not do it. And yet he is the one representative of the whole people, their trustee."

Or consider such an utterance as this from the *Kansas City Star* of April 11, 1910: —

"The country wants the administration to 'make good.' The people would far rather think well than ill of the President. But they can have no confidence in his program until the results are shown, and then they will not accept it if it is punched with loopholes and punctuated with jokers at the hands of the interest-serving leaders on whom the President is relying."

How, with such relations between the President and Congress as now exist, can he prevent such punching and punctuation? Hamilton mentioned as political "axioms as simple as they are universal," that "the means ought to be proportioned to the end; the persons, from whose agency the attainment of any end is expected, ought to possess the means by which it is to be attained." [1] Is it not plain that the only means that can accomplish the end expected of the President is that he shall have charge of his measures while they are under discussion, so that proposed amendments shall be subjected to his expositions of their significance? That is exactly the way in which the public business is transacted in Switzerland. Bills are in charge of the

[1] *The Federalist*, No. 23.

administration and all changes which may be ordered by Congress after discussion are drafted by the administration. No opportunity is allowed for punching loopholes or slipping in jokers through parliamentary cunning.

Such utterance as I have quoted is very significant, since in the long run it is the stress of political necessity that makes and unmakes constitutional deposits of authority. By an ordinary law of political development the function thus impressed upon the presidential office must eventually acquire institutional forms of activity. The obvious solution is by a connection of the powers. The administration should have the right to present its measures in the form it thinks advisable, explain and defend them before the Houses of Congress, and the powers heretofore exercised by the House Committee of Rules should be vested in it for that purpose. Then Congress, relieved from the administrative details over which it now mulls, would become a deliberative body, and would rise in real power and true dignity. All these things are involved in the present tendencies of American politics, but it may require much bitter experience — perhaps great national disasters — before the opposition of class privilege and particular interests to such changes as these can be overcome. Great constitutional improvements do not come about through acquiescence but through compulsion.

I am getting pretty far afield, but I cannot too strongly emphasize my belief that the laws which control the fate of institutions and the destinies of nations will not be suspended in favor of the United States.

Unless Congress can be brought into subordination to the general welfare it is doomed. That is why I said that the action taken by Congress making it the duty of the President to coördinate income and expenditure is the salvation of representative government in the United States. The logical significance of this action is that the numerous pass-keys to the national treasury now held by congressional committees must be given up and that there shall be but one key, which shall be in the custody of the President. Upon the creation of just such a situation as that the efficiency of representative government depends. Its essential principle is to fix the representatives so that they cannot put their own hands into the till; then they will keep a good watch over those who do handle the money. Congressmen will take a very different view of pork-barrels from that now held when they can no longer help themselves to the pork.

Observe how the new rule is beginning to work. President Taft in his message of December 9, 1909, reported that as a result of the new method of making up the estimates departmental demands had been curtailed so that the estimates transmitted to Congress were less than the appropriations for the fiscal year then current by $42,818,000. But it would be obviously futile to prepare estimates if they may be crossed by other estimates privately transmitted to Congress by department officials. So executive order No. 1142 was issued as follows: —

"It is hereby ordered that no bureau officer or division chief or subordinate in any department of the Government and no officer of the army or navy or Marine Corps stationed in Washington shall apply to either house of Congress or to any committee of either house of Congress, or to any member of Congress, for legislation or for appropriations or for Congressional action of any kind except with the consent and knowledge of the head of the Department; nor shall any such person respond to any request for information from either house of Congress or any committee of either house of Congress or any member of Congress, except through or as authorized by the head of his department."

This necessary restraint upon individual interference by Congressmen with executive function at once evoked protests. According to a Washington dispatch in the *New York Sun* of December 1, 1909: "Those Senators and Representatives who have read the text of the order are up in arms over it, saying that it abridges rights and privileges that members of Congress have had conceded for fifty years or more." Despite the disagreeable obstruction which the order puts in the way of Congressmen when acting as special agents for interests engaging their service, the enforcement of it is unavoidable if the public expenditure is to be brought under the control of public motive and restricted to public account. The proper place for intelligence between the executive departments and Congress is on the floor of Congress, through the presence of the heads of the departments, as in Switzerland.

Consideration will show that pursuance of the duty of budget supervision now resting upon the President will require far more energetic exertion of his constitutional authority than is manifested by executive order No. 1142. The estimates as prepared by the heads of departments under executive supervision will be illusory, if Congress itself may issue orders directly to heads of departments for the preparation of estimates without consulting the President. This very thing Congress does by the device known as the concurrent resolution, a legislative act which is not laid before the President, but which nevertheless directs the Secretary of the Treasury and the Secretary of War to frame the estimates on which the appropriations are made for public buildings and for river and harbor improvements. However submissive and deferential individual incumbents may be, sooner or later the budget responsibilities of the presidential office will incite some action to repel this invasion of its constitutional prerogative. The President ought not to allow any of the executive departments to treat concurrent resolutions as of any legal force or effect.

Another matter which the pressure of the President's budget responsibility must eventually make acute is supervision of the items of appropriation bills. His estimates will be of small practical importance if Congress may exceed them at pleasure and require him to spend more than he thinks necessary or judicious. It is a frequent occurrence for the Senate to pad the appropriation bills of a session by much more than the amount of the reduction which has been made by the President in submitting the estimates. Is the President bound to accept and spend money against his will and judgment? Take the case of that item of $47,000 in 1903 which was denounced in the House as "legislative blackmail," but which was acquiesced in to avert the failure of the bill.[1] Is the President likewise helpless? Is there no power anywhere in our constitutional system able to cope with such an emer-

[1] See *ante*, p. 27.

gency? The logical corollary to the budget responsibility laid upon the President is that he shall apply his veto power to the items of appropriation bills. Any movement in that direction would, of course, raise a constitutional issue of profound importance, in which much could and would be said on both sides. Beyond some mention of historical circumstances, I shall not afflict you with a foretaste of such a discussion now. The issue when it arises will be determined by preponderance of political force, and much will depend upon the circumspection of the President who faces that issue. A President in conjunction with the House can beat the Senate to its knees; but it will be a dubious contention should he attempt to withstand both houses of Congress. There is a natural affinity between the President and the House which under proper cultivation should provide facilities for joint action. If, for instance, the President had vetoed that $47,000 item denounced by the House, what could the Senate have done to uphold it?

If ever the constitutional lawyers get to work on this question they will doubtless dig up precedents now unnoted. A clause of the Constitution which would be sure to figure largely in such a discussion is the last clause of Sec. 7, Art. 1, to which I have adverted several times in these lectures. It requires that "every order, resolution, or vote, to which concurrence of the Senate and House of Representatives may be necessary (except on a question of adjournment) shall be presented to the President of the United States." The exception gives remarkable breadth to the rule. If it does not really bring votes within the scope of executive examination, what does it mean? It is a significant fact that in English parliamentary practice the different classes of appropriations are known as "votes."[1] If it is a case of take all or nothing when the appropriation bills reach the President, he may be put under a duress that practically annuls his constitutional rights. In a message of August 14, 1876, President Grant claimed discretionary authority over the items of appropriation bills, and a like doctrine was propounded by Senator John Sherman in the course of a debate on the river and harbor bill on June 3, 1896. He declared that appropriations were not mandatory, but simply permissive. "If the President of the United States should see proper to say 'That object of appropriation is not a wise one; I do not concur that the money ought to be expended,' that is the end of it." It is safe to say that the great invasion of executive function that has been accomplished by Congress will not be repelled save by Jacksonian vigor in the use of all the resources of presidential authority. They are ample for the purpose when skilfully and energetically applied, and the nature of this budget problem is such as to demand their use. It is possible for a President to put legislation through Congress by private persuasion and entreaty, and by starting a back fire to smoke out committee hiding-places by means of speech-making to the people, although the legislation will be apt to be botched in character, and his speech-making will be depreciated in quality by accommodation to the conditions of the stump, which

[1] See Redlich's "Procedure of the House of Commons," Vol. III, p. 139.

are far different from those of the legislative forum. But he cannot keep down expenses in that way, for his dependence upon congressional favor for consideration of his measures must tend to procure such indulgence as to appropriations as will keep Congress in good humor.[1] As Washington observed, "Influence is not government." Responsible government will not arise until it can exist by right.

Thus it appears that this question of the cost of government involves the whole organization of public authority. The establishment of budget control involves the connection of the powers of government. To effect that connection the present rule of privileged interests must be overthrown. Committee government must be superseded by responsible government. That means a hard struggle, but it is inevitable, and the signs of the times indicate that the people are quite ready for it and are craving effective leadership.

[1] Since this statement was made it has been verified by the appropriations made by the 61st Congress, 2d session, ending June 25, 1910. A tabulated exhibit of the appropriations, compared with the executive estimates, is given in appendix D.

APPENDIX A

Analysis of Public Expenditures

The following document was prepared for the House Committee on Appropriations by the Bureau of the Census, and was appended to the annual review of appropriations and expenditures by Chairman Tawney, published in the Congressional Record for May 30, 1908.

The figure given in the column "ratio" is the quotient secured by dividing the per capita expenditures of the period under consideration by the corresponding per capita for the years from 1791 to 1796.

Table 1. — *A.* — *Total and Per Capita Expenditures of the National Government for all Purposes for Specified Periods*, 1791–1907

Period	Average Annual Expenditures	Per Capita Annual Expenditures	
		Amount	Ratio
1791–1796	$5,854,172	$1.34	1.00
1821–1828	17,681,344	1.59	1.19
1846–1853	49,137,138	2.23	1.66
1878–1885	294,855,816	5.66	4.22
1898–1905	653,932,414	8.17	6.10
1906	736,717,502	8.72	6.51
1907	762,488,752	8.91	6.65

B.—Paid from General Revenues for Specified Periods, 1791–1907

Period	Average Annual Expenditures	Per Capita Average Expenditures	
		Amount	Ratio
1791–1796	$5,852,509	$1.32	1.00
1821–1828	16,407,424	1.47	1.11
1846–1853	44,266,671	2.02	1.53
1878–1885	257,019,281	4.93	3.73
1898–1905	521,636,626	6.65	5.00
1906	568,784,799	6.73	5.10
1907	578,903,746	6.77	5.13

C.—For the United States Post-office for Specified Periods, 1791–1907

Period	Average Annual Expenditures	Per Capita Annual Expenditures			
		Paid from Postal Revenues	Paid from General Revenues	Total	
				Amount	Ratio
1791–1796	$83,784	$0.02	—	$0.02	1.00
1821–1828	1,273,916	.12	—	.12	6.00
1846–1853	5,390,961	.21	$0.02	.23	11.50
1878–1885	41,638,131	.73	.07	.80	40.00
1898–1905	126,608,377	1.54	.10	1.62	81.00
1906	180,606,077	1.99	.15	2.14	107.00
1907	191,214,389	2.15	.09	2.24	112.00

The expenditures in not only the federal government but all state and local governments are met in part from public taxes and in part from other revenues. In the federal government the latter class comprises principally revenues received as compensation for services rendered by the Post-office.

The postal expenditures in 1907 were 112 times greater than those of the six years of Washington's administration for which the table presents data. Comparison of the expenditures for postal service in 1907 with similar expenditures in 1791 (but $36,697) shows that such expenditure increased 248 times as rapidly as population, while all governmental expenditures increased about 6.3 times.

The increase of national expenditures actually met from taxation is reflected fairly well by the figures given above, although the reported expenditures include payments for other purposes than the cost of government and payments that are not met from the proceeds of national taxation. Among the payments of the first class so included are those for the expenditures of the District of Columbia disbursed through the national treasury, the payments of trust moneys, and duplications of many kinds. Among the payments of the second class are those for governmental expenditures which are met from fees for services, such as those of the Patent Office and of the General Land Office. The payments for both of these classes, like the expenditures of the Post-office, have increased much faster than the expenditures met from public taxation. The data for an exact exhibit of these payments are, however, not readily available. If they were, it would be found that the actual increase of expenditures payable from national taxes was slightly less than indicated by the table.

Expenditures with Relation to Population

National expenditures payable from taxes have increased in one hundred and eleven years something over five times as fast as population. The relative increase was much slower in the first sixty years of national life than in the last fifty. The greatest increase was in the period which includes the Civil War, and largely represents the increase in the governmental payments for interest and pensions. Just prior to the Civil War these payments were only 13 cents per capita per annum. This was the lowest in the national history, and was less than one fifth the corresponding per capita payment of 1796 to 1800. The per capita annual payments for interest and pensions in the four years ending June 30, 1869, were $4.32, and by 1907 had declined to $1.92. This decline was balanced by a relative increase of other costs of government, so that in 1907 the per capita for all expenditures payable from taxes was not far from five times what it was in Washington's time. The same statement can also be made of all such expenditures, exclusive of those for interest and pensions.

The average annual per capita expenditures of the national government payable from taxes for the eight years 1846 to 1853 was $2.02; for the eight years ending June 30, 1905, it was $6.65; and for the year ending June 30, 1907, $6.77. The average for the eight years 1898 to 1905 was 3.29 times, and that for 1907 was 3.35 times, the corresponding average for the period 1846 to 1853. To the extent represented by these numbers did the expenditures payable from taxes increase faster than population.

Expenditures with Relation to National Wealth

The per capita of national taxable wealth was $308 in 1850 and $1234 in 1904. In the latter year it was four times what it was in 1850, indicating that the relative ability of the nation to pay taxes had increased in fifty-four years four times, while the national expenditures payable from taxes had increased in the fifty-seven years ending in 1907 only 3.35 times. The national wealth, or the ability to meet governmental expenditures, increased at least 20 and possibly 25 per cent more than did the national expenditures to be met from taxation. Considering the number of people in the country to be taxed, the present national administration makes the government 3.35 times as costly to the taxpayer as did the government of 1846 to 1853. But taking account of the wealth of the citizens or their ability to support the government, the administration of the United States in 1907 was only 75 or 80 per cent as burdensome as that which controlled the country at the middle of the last century.

Increase in the Expenditures of the National Government as Compared with those of State, Municipal, and Local Governments

The following table presents the actual expenditures of the federal government by decades, from 1850 to 1907, a period of fifty-seven years, and the amount which such expenditures repre-

Total National Wealth and Expenditures of the Federal Government and of State, County, Municipal, and all Local Governments, per $1000 of Wealth, 1860–1907

Year	Total National Wealth	Total Expenditures of National Government (taxable)		Tax Levy for Expenditures for States, Counties, Cities, Minor Civil Divisions, including Schools		Payment for Expenditures for States, Counties, Cities, Minor Civil Divisions, including Schools	
		Amount	Per $1000 of National Wealth	Amount	Per $1000 of National Wealth	Amount	Per $1000 of National Wealth
1850	$7,135,780,228	$46,448,368	$6.5	—	—	—	—
1860	16,159,616,068	71,718,943	4.4	$94,186,746	$5.8	—	—
1870	24,054,814,806	313,429,226	13.2	226,185,629	9.4	—	—
1880	41,067,122,000	298,163,117	7.3	313,921,474	7.6	—	—
1890	61,203,755,972	358,618,585	5.9	471,365,140	7.7	$569,252,634	$9.3
1900	82,304,517,845	590,068,371	7.2	—	—	—	—
1902	[1] 91,238,732,842	593,038,905	6.5	724,736,539	7.9	1,156,447,085	12.8
1904	100,272,947,840	725,984,946	7.2	—	—	—	—
1907	[1] 113,947,270,337	762,488,752	6.7	—	—	—	—

[1] Estimated on basis of increase 1900–1904.

sent per $1000 of national wealth as compiled at the various census periods mentioned. The proportion per $1000 of national wealth of the taxes levied to meet the expenditure, including schools, for government other than federal, from 1860 to 1902, and the grand total of expenditure for government, exclusive of federal, compiled only at the Eleventh and Twelfth Censuses, are also presented.

The expenditures of the national government payable from taxation may be compared with the general property taxes levied for the support of state and municipal governments. The tax levies for state and municipal governments were ascertained by the Bureau of the Census for 1880, 1890, and 1902. For 1880 the per capita of such levies was $6.26, and in 1902, $9.22. In twenty-two years it increased 47.3 per cent. The per capita of national expenditures payable from taxation in 1880 was $5.28, and in 1902, $5.91, and in 1907, $6.77. The percentage of increase from 1880 to 1902 was 12, and from 1880 to 1907 only 28.2. The former was only a fourth and the latter barely 60 per cent of the corresponding percentage of increase of state and local taxation for twenty-two years. State and local taxation is increasing proportionately with national wealth and the ability of the people to meet the added costs of local government, while national expenditures — though growing rapidly — do not keep pace with the increasing national wealth; and so the burden of national government becomes smaller and smaller with the passing of the decades — at least, that has been the general trend of affairs since the middle of the nineteenth century, in spite of the cost of the Civil War with its legacy of heavy interest and pension charges.

APPENDIX B

Budget Procedure in the House of Representatives

In answer to an application from the author, the following account of Budget Procedure was furnished, under date of October 13, 1909, by the Hon. James A. Tawney, Chairman of the Committee on Appropriations: —

"Prior to the enactment of Section 7 of the sundry civil appropriation act, approved March 4, 1909, the law only required the heads of the several executive departments of the government to submit their estimates for the next fiscal year's expenditures to the Secretary of the Treasury on or before October 15th of each year. It was then made the regular duty of the Secretary of the Treasury to arrange and compile these estimates thus submitted, have them printed, and transmit the same to Congress on the opening day of the session. Under this law, and the practices which it authorized, the head of each department prepared his estimates, or the estimates for his department, without any reference whatever to the estimates submitted by the heads of the other departments, and without any reference whatever to the estimated revenues for the fiscal year for which the estimated expenditures were to be made. The law also required the Secretary of the Treasury, in submitting the estimates for expenditures for appropriations to also submit an estimate of the probable revenues. Under this practice the estimates for appropriations were made without any reference to the estimated revenues, and frequently these estimates for appropriations were far in excess of the estimated revenues. This threw upon the Committee on Appropriations the necessity of reducing the estimated expenditures so as to keep the appropriations within the estimated revenues.

"Section 7 of the sundry civil appropriation act referred to, provides as follows: —

"'Immediately upon the receipt of the regular annual estimates of appropriations needed for the various branches of the government, it shall be the duty of the Secretary of the Treasury to estimate as nearly as may be the revenues of the government for the ensuing fiscal year, and if the estimates for appropriations, including the estimated amount necessary to meet all continuing and permanent appropriations, shall exceed the estimated revenues, the Secretary of the Treasury shall transmit the estimates to Congress as heretofore required by law and at once transmit a detailed statement of all of said estimates to the President, to the end that he may, in giving Congress information of the state of the Union and in recommending to their consideration such measures as he may judge necessary, advise Congress how in his judgment the estimated appropriations could, with least injury to the public service, be reduced so as to bring the appropriations within the estimated revenues, or, if such reduction be not in his judgment practicable without undue injury to the public service, that he may recommend to Congress such loans or new taxes as may be necessary to cover the deficiency.'

"From this you will observe that if the budgets hereafter submitted exceed in the aggregate the estimated revenues, the President must either recommend to Congress what estimated expenditures can be omitted without detriment to the public service, so as to bring the appropriations within the estimated revenues, or else recommend to Congress new sources of taxation from which the deficit can be made up. The existence of the responsibility thus created has prompted President Taft to organize a committee of his cabinet to go over the estimates before the same are submitted to the Secretary of the Treasury in accordance with the law and thereby correlate all the estimated expenditures so as to bring the same within the estimated revenues. This will greatly relieve the committees of the House of Representatives which have appropriating jurisdiction so far as the estimates of the executive departments are concerned. Hitherto it has been the practice for each department to resist any proposed reduction in their estimates in order to bring the total appropriations within the estimated revenues.

"One of the greatest evils that to-day exist in our system of submitting estimates and making appropriations for public expenditures is the divided jurisdiction over appropriations. This jurisdiction is divided between eight committees of the House. Seven of these committees have jurisdiction over but one appropriation bill, and that is the bill carrying the appropriations for one particular executive department. The Agricultural Committee has charge of the agricultural appropriation bill; the Naval Committee, of the naval appropriation bill; the Committee on Military Affairs, of the army appropriation bill and military academy appropriation bill; the Post-office Committee, of the post-office appropriation bill; the Foreign Affairs Committee, of the diplomatic and consular appropriation bill; the Committee on Indian Affairs, of the Indian appropriation bill; and the River and Harbor Committee, of appropriations for river and harbor improvements, except those improvements which are authorized to be made under continuing contracts.

"The Committee on Appropriations has jurisdiction over appropriations for legislative, executive, and judicial expenditures, which are carried in one bill; the District of Columbia appropriation bill; the fortification appropriation bill; the pension appropriation bill; the sundry civil appropriation bill; and all deficiency appropriation bills.

"Each of those committees which has jurisdiction of but one appropriation bill naturally becomes the partisan representative of the department for which it recommends appropriations rather than the representative of the body to which its members belong and which is ultimately responsible for the appropriations which are made for that department. When, in the Forty-fourth Congress, under the leadership of Carlisle and Morrison, the jurisdiction of the Committee on Appropriations was thus divided, for the purpose of weakening the influence of Samuel J. Randall, a protectionist Democrat, Mr. Randall and Mr. Cannon, now Speaker, then members of that committee, predicted that this division of jurisdiction would cost the people of the United States not less than $50,000,000 annually. They were not far out of the way, as our experience has proven.

"In my judgment this is one of the chief causes for the rapid increase in our appropriations for public expenditures. If the jurisdiction over appropriations were vested in one committee, as it was prior to this time, it would not have been possible during the last eight years to have increased the annual appropriations for the army from $24,000,000, the average annual appropriation for the army for the eight years preceding the Spanish-American War, to $83,000,000, the average annual appropriation for the eight years last past, including the present fiscal year, 1910; nor would it have been possible to have increased the appropriation of the navy from $27,500,000, the average annual appropriation for the same period prior to the Spanish-American War, to more than an average of $102,400,000, for the eight years last past, including the current fiscal year, 1910. Nor would the increase for other departments, for which appropriations are made by individual committees, be as great; nor would we have had the deficit in our revenues during the past two years we have had.

"Whether this defect will ever be remedied or not, I am unable to say. It cannot be done unless it is the result of a great popular demand, for the reason that these seven committees, which have a membership of nineteen each, would combine to prevent the House from taking away from them jurisdiction over particular appropriation bills which they now possess. It may be that the effect of Section 7 of the sundry civil appropriation bill will to some extent check the increase in appropriations for these departments for which these different committees recommend appropriations. It was my thought in securing the enactment of this section that we might possibly check the rapid increase in such appropriations by the adoption of this section.

"The plan which the President has adopted under this section throws upon the head of each department the responsibility for his aggregate estimates with reference to the combined aggregate estimates for all the departments; and in this way the one may keep the other down to the minimum.

"When the estimates are submitted to Congress, they are referred by the Speaker of the House to the several committees having jurisdiction over particular appropriations for which the estimates are made. The practice is then for these committees to send for the heads of the departments, the bureau chiefs in the department, and have them fully explain to the committee the necessity for the appropriations for which estimates are made. At these hearings these officers are closely examined by the committee regarding the subject-matter of their estimates and after such examination the committee then makes up its bill, recommending the amount which in its judgment should be appropriated under each particular head.

"The rule differs somewhat in the Committee on Appropriations, for that committee has jurisdiction over five general appropriation bills and all of the deficiency appropriation bills. The Committee on Appropriations is divided into seven subcommittees, the seventh one having jurisdiction over permanent appropriations. But owing to the legislation making these permanent appropriations this subcommittee has nothing to do. Each subcommittee considers the estimates for expenditures under the appropriation bill over which it has jurisdiction, and when the bill is finally prepared by the subcommittee it is reported to the full committee and the full committee recommends to the House the passage of the bill as prepared and submitted by the committee.

"Outside of the demands for appropriations which come to Congress through the regular estimates, we have what is known as supplemental estimates; and prior to the 59th Congress the practice was to submit a large part of the estimates for appropriations through supplemental estimates. This practice grew out of the carelessness of the departments in making their general estimates covering all of the needs of their respective departments for the year for which the estimates were made. That is, after the general estimates were submitted and Congress was in session, they would discover that they had neglected to estimate for certain appropriations and would then submit them in the form of a supplemental estimate. This practice I endeavored to check by making it unlawful to submit a supplemental estimate except on account of some expenditure authorized by the session of Congress to which the regular estimates had been submitted, or on account of the happening of some emergency which could not be anticipated at the time of preparing and submitting the regular estimates.

"In addition to the supplemental estimates, demands for appropriations come from the recommendations of the board of engineers of the War Department to the Committee on Rivers and Harbors. Their recommendations are made in connection with reports on investigations for river and harbor improvements, which investigations are usually made under the direction of Congress. Hence, the appropriations made upon the report of the engineers of the War Department are not usually carried in the regular estimates.

"Another source of appropriations is in the authorizations for appropriations carried in legislation which is enacted during the session; that is, if a bill authorizing a service passes and becomes a law, it then becomes necessary to appropriate the money for carrying into effect this law or providing for the service which it creates. So that the sources from which emanate the demands for appropriations are: first, the regular annual estimates, submitted by the Secretary of the Treasury at the beginning of each session of Congress, including the estimates of all the executive departments of the government; second, the supplemental and deficiency estimates; third, the reports of the engineers of the War Department for river and harbor improvements; and fourth, new authorizations or authorizations enacted at the session of Congress for which the annual appropriations are made, including appropriations for the payment of claims allowed under the Bowman act or recommended under the Tucker act.

"The demands that are made by individual members of Congress and senators upon the Committee on Appropriations, independent of the regular and supplemental estimates, are very few and are never granted unless the appropriation asked for has been previously authorized by law, or unless the House by unanimous consent includes such a demand in one of the appropriation bills, for under the rules of the House no appropriation can be considered, except by unanimous consent, unless such appropriation has been previously authorized by law.

"The difficulty in practice which the Committee on Appropriations has in trying to keep the appropriations within the estimated revenues arises from the fact that the several committees which have jurisdiction over the appropriations for a particular department appropriate for the field service only of that department, or for the naval or military establishments. That is, their appropriations are entirely for the service outside of the city of Washington over which the respective departments have jurisdiction, or for the naval or military establishments outside of the Navy and War Departments at Washington. These appropriations being expended out in the districts and states represented by members of the House and Senate, the departments for which the appropriations are made can always rely upon the representatives and senators in whose districts and states these appropriations are to be expended to support almost any demand they make; and it has not been an uncommon thing for the bureau chiefs to line up or to lobby with the representatives and senators in whose districts or states the appropriations are to be expended for the purpose of securing their support on the floor of either House. I have even known bureau chiefs to prepare briefs and arguments for members to be made on the floor of the House in support of proposed increases in appropriations recommended by the Committee on Appropriations. But I am glad to say that as the result of efforts of myself and my associates on the Committee on Appropriations this practice has been almost completely done away with. It obtains yet to some extent, but it is not done as openly as it used to be.

"I know it is a popular impression that members of the House and Senate demand appropriations upon their own responsibility, but this is not the fact. As I said before, they do it occasionally, but it is only where the appropriation asked for has been previously authorized by law. The clamor on the part of members and senators for appropriations is in support of appropriations which are estimated for regularly by the departments or included in supplemental estimates; and their motive, as I have also stated, is the fact that the money is to be expended in the field service of the government, or in the navy yards or at the military posts in the districts or states which the members or senators represent."

APPENDIX C

Post-Office Appropriations

The following is the essential portion of a communication received from former Postmaster-General Meyer, under date of February 26, 1909: —

"It is the opinion of the Department that in the large cities buildings should be constructed exclusively for post-office use, especially designed for that purpose, and located in the immediate vicinity of the union railroad stations, so that the cost of transporting the mails between the post-offices and the stations may be saved and the distribution facilitated. At the urgent solicitation of the Department, Congress has acquired a site for a new post-office building in Washington, immediately adjacent to the new Union Station, and an appropriation has been secured for a new post-office building in the city of Chicago, the purpose being to locate it as near as possible to the principal railway stations where the mails are received and despatched. A post-office building is also in process of construction in the city of New York immediately above the terminal station of the Pennsylvania Railroad Company. A site has also been secured for a new post-office building in the city of Saint Louis and plans are now being perfected for the construction of a building, the site adjoining the Union Station.

"As a general rule, however, in the preparation of the Public Buildings bills the executive branch of the government is not consulted with respect to making appropriations for the new public buildings. At the last session of Congress more than twenty millions of dollars were appropriated for the construction of public buildings for the exclusive use of post-offices in the smaller cities and towns, where the Department had made no recommendation for new buildings. The initial cost of public buildings, together with the cost of maintenance, is very much in excess of the amount required to provide suitable rented quarters properly equipped for post-office purposes in the smaller cities and towns, and from the standpoint of economy, therefore, there are no arguments worthy of consideration in favor of public buildings in these towns. On the other hand, the federal building represents the government, and if it stimulates national and civic pride, and if love of country and patriotism are thus instilled in the minds of the people, the money is no doubt well expended."

APPENDIX D

EXECUTIVE ESTIMATES AND CONGRESSIONAL APPROPRIATIONS

As a result of the lack of budget system in the United States, there is always room for dispute as to the amount of the expenditure authorized by the appropriation bills. Various partisan statements are made at the close of every congressional session, differing as to amounts. For the purposes of this work, it has been thought sufficient to give the statements of the chairmen of the Appropriations committees of the House and the Senate, along with the estimates transmitted by the Secretary of the Treasury. For additional details the reader may consult the Congressional Record, vol. 45, 61st Congress, 2d session, Nos. 163, 164.

The arrangement by fiscal years is such that the duty imposed upon the President by the Act of March 4, 1909, could not be discharged with any marked effect prior to the preparation of the estimates for the fiscal year of 1911. These, as transmitted by the Secretary of the Treasury (report for 1909, page 26), were as follows: —

EXECUTIVE ESTIMATE

Legislative establishment		$7,093,201.00
Executive establishment —		
Executive proper	$472,270.00	
Department of State	299,720.00	

Treasury Department . . .	11,220,515.00	
War Department	2,272,908.00	
Navy Department	841,500.00	
Department of Interior . . .	5,044,745.00	
Post-Office Department . . .	1,695,690.00	
Department of Agriculture . .	13,377,136.00	
Department of Commerce and Labor	3,431,330.00	
Department of Justice . . .	525,740.00	
Territorial governments . . .	266,850.00	
		39,448,404.00
Judicial establishment		1,072,600.00
Foreign intercourse		4,133,581.41
Military establishment		95,605,147.92
Naval establishment		108,106,264.38
Indian affairs		8,988,262.90
Pensions		155,858,000.00
Public works —		
Legislative	7,000.00	
Treasury Department . . .	7,028,365.60	
War Department	39,983,392.38	
Navy Department	5,957,150.00	
Department of Interior . . .	246,000.00	
Department of Commerce and Labor	223,200.00	
Department of Justice . . .	275,000.00	
		53,720,107.98
Miscellaneous —		
Legislative	6,009,478.70	
Treasury Department . . .	20,383,725.00	
War Department	6,700,072.98	
Department of Interior . . .	4,509,175.00	
Department of Commerce and Labor	9,935,383.00	
Department of Justice . . .	7,502,800.00	
District of Columbia	11,180,628.49	
Smithsonian Institution and National Museum	974,000.00	

Interstate Commerce Commission	1,370,000.00	
		68,565,263.17
Postal deficiency		10,634,122.63
Permanent annual appropriations —		
Interest on the public debt . .	22,195,000.00	
Refunds — customs, internal revenue, etc.	19,144,300.00	
Collecting revenue from customs	5,500,000.00	
Miscellaneous, exclusive of sinking fund and national-bank note redemption account . .	23,160,295.12	
		69,999,595.12
		623,224,550.51
Add estimated naval appropriations for new ships for expenditure the first year, received from the Secretary of the Navy after completion of the Book of Estimates and to be separately transmitted to Congress		12,844,122.00
Total estimated ordinary appropriations, excluding postal service payable from the postal revenues, but including the postal deficiency		636,068,672.51
The Panama Canal appropriations to be met by sales of bonds are estimated at		48,063,524.70
Total estimated appropriations for 1911 .		684,132,197.21

Congressional Appropriations

Statement by Mr. Hale, chairman of the Senate Committee on Appropriations

Title	Fiscal Year 1909	Fiscal Year 1910	Fiscal Year 1911
Agriculture	$11,672,106.00	$12,995,036.00	$13,487,636.00
Army	95,382,247.61	101,195,883.34	95,440,567.55
Diplomatic and consular	3,538,852.72	3,613,861.67	4,116,081.41
District of Columbia	10,001,888.85	10,699,531.49	10,608,045.99
Fortifications	9,316,745.00	8,170,111.00	5,617,200.00
Indian	9,253,347.87	11,854,982.48	9,266,528.00
Legislative, etc.	32,832,913.50	32,007,049.00	34,158,767.00
Military Academy	845,634.87	2,531,521.33	1,856,249.87
Navy	122,663,885.47	136,935,199.05	131,350,854.38
Pension	163,053,000.00	160,908,000.00	155,758,000.00
Post-office	222,970,892.00	234,692,370.00	243,907,020.00
River and harbor	—	9,435,750.00	41,329,113.50
Sundry civil	111,958,088.23	137,696,623.36	113,984,101.82
Total	793,489,602.12	862,735,918.72	860,880,165.52
Deficiency, 1910 and prior years	56,702,309.06	20,310,339.92	12,722,739.80
Total	850,191,911.18	883,046,258.64	873,602,905.32
Miscellaneous	4,011,337.26	12,520,926.72	2,000,000.00
Reclamation projects	—	—	20,000,000.00
Total, regular annual appropriations	854,203,248.44	895,567,185.36	895,602,905.32
Permanent annual appropriations	154,194,295.12	160,096,082.52	130,934,595.12
Grand total, regular and permanent annual appropriations	1,008,397,543.56	1,055,663,267.88	1,026,537,500.44

Statement by Mr. Tawney, chairman of the House Committee on Appropriations

Title	Reported to the House	Passed the House	Reported to the Senate	Passed the Senate	Law, 1910–11
Agriculture	$13,417,136.00	$13,330,276.00	$13,512,636.00	$13,522,636.00	$13,487,636.00
Army	95,322,707.55	95,297,707.55	95,440,567.55	95,440,567.55	95,440,567.55
Diplomatic and consular	3,986,981.41	3,731,981.41	4,119,481.41	4,166,081.41	4,116,081.41
District of Columbia	10,285,907.99	10,258,067.99	10,946,960.99	11,012,960.99	10,608,045.99
Fortification	5,617,200.00	5,617,200.00	5,817,200.00	5,817,200.00	5,617,200.00
Indian	8,513,757.90	8,798,478.00	9,920,934.68	9,931,934.68	9,266,528.00
Legislative, etc.	33,897,815.00	33,853,295.00	34,044,357.00	34,207,017.00	34,158,767.00
Military academy	1,855,249.87	1,855,249.87	1,856,649.87	1,856,649.87	1,856,249.87
Navy	129,037,602.93	127,829,602.93	130,737,934.38	131,679,854.38	131,350,854.38
Pension	155,674,000.00	155,674,000.00	155,758,000.00	155,758,000.00	155,758,000 00
Post-office	239,812,195.00	243,907,020.00	243,907,020.00	243,907,020.00	243,907,020.00
River and harbor	35,173,846.50	35,351,746.50	41,732,313.50	41,819,113.50	41,329,113.50
Sundry civil	111,804,838.82	112,302,541.82	117,408,970.02	117,618,320.02	114,080,101.82
Total	844,399,238.97	847,807,167.07	865,203,025.40	866,737,355.40	860,976,165.52
Urgent deficiency, 1910 and prior years	5,013,836.03	5,116,325.73	5,713,124.79	5,768,409.65	5,767,699.22
Deficiency, 1910 and prior years	5,737,412.09	6,264,601.47	7,946,946.58	8,338,490.14	6,954,986.58
Total	855,150,487.09	859,188,094.27	878,863,096.77	880,844,255.19	873,698,851.32
Miscellaneous	—	—	—	—	2,500,000.00
Advances to reclamation fund, reimbursable from receipts of reclamation fund	—	—	—	—	20,000,000.00
Total, regular annual appropriations	—	—	—	—	896,198,851.32
Permanent annual appropriations	—	—	—	—	130,934,595.12
Grand total, regular and permanent annual appropriations	—	—	—	—	1,027,133,446.44

Remarks

In comparing the executive estimates with the congressional appropriations, allowance should be made for the fact that the Secretary of the Treasury does not include post-office receipts in his estimates, but only the postal deficiency. In the statement of appropriations the post-office receipts are included in the amount of the appropriation, which was made on the assumption that $233,058,572 would be supplied by postal revenues. Adding this amount to the estimates transmitted by the Secretary of the Treasury, the total is raised to $917,190,769, as against appropriations made by Congress for that fiscal year amounting to $1,026,537,500, according to Senator Hale's statement, or $1,027,133,446, according to Representative Tawney's statement.

Detailed comparison between the estimates and the appropriations is impossible, because the appropriations are not accurately classified, and the cost of any particular service may be scattered through various appropriation bills. Demands successfully resisted when one bill is under consideration may be slipped into another bill. For instance, when the Legislative Appropriation bill was under consideration in the Senate, March 24, 1910, an item appropriating $1800, for the salary of a professional masseur was so severely criticized that it was dropped.[1] But on June 21 the masseur was provided for by an item inserted in the Deficiency Appropriation bill, appropriating $1800 to pay the salary of an "attendant in charge of the bath-

[1] See *ante*, page 92.

ing rooms in the Senate Office Building." Conditions are such that it is impossible to ascertain the exact cost of any branch of the public service. In this respect the contrast between congressional appropriations and those made by the British Parliament is very striking. In the latter, the cost of every public office is exactly set forth. I have at hand the estimates for 1907. They are grouped in seven classes, and the subclasses of each group are numbered, with a page reference, on turning to which one finds full particulars as to the expenditures under that head, including the number and pay of employes. In addition, a full index is provided, to which one may turn for reference to any item on which information is desired. As an example of the completeness of this index I give a small extract from the entries under the letter A, as follows: —

	PAGE
Aberystwith University College, Wales	398
Academy Royal, of Music, England	395
of Music, Ireland	396
Hibernian, Ireland	396
Irish, Ireland	395
Irish, Buildings	69
Accidents (Railways) Act, Expenses under	119
Accountant of Court, Scotland	290
Accounting Office, Consolidated, Supreme Court of Judicature, Ireland	315
Admiralty Registry (see Supreme Court), England	241
Admiralty Marshal, England	241
Admiralty Court Registrar, Ireland	314
Admiralty Buildings	46
Advocate, Lord, Scotland	286
Africa, British Protectorates in	463

Fourteen long pages are occupied by a minute index of this character, set in double columns. There is nothing like this in our budget statements. Compared with the exact and minute system of English budget control, our methods seem like the ignorant and disorderly practices of barbarians.

INDEX

THE COLUMBIA UNIVERSITY PRESS

Columbia University in the City of New York

The Press was incorporated June 8, 1893, to promote the publication of the results of original research. It is a private corporation, related directly to Columbia University by the provisions that its Trustees shall be officers of the University and that the President of Columbia University shall be President of the Press.

The publications of the Columbia University Press include works on Biography, History, Economics, Education, Philosophy, Linguistics, and Literature, and the following series:

Columbia University Biological Series.

Columbia University Studies in Classical Philology.

Columbia University Studies in Comparative Literature.

Columbia University Studies in English.

Columbia University Geological Series.

Columbia University Germanic Studies.

Columbia University Indo-Iranian Series.

Columbia University Contributions to Oriental History and Philology.

Columbia University Oriental Studies.

Columbia University Studies in Romance Philology and Literature.

Blumenthal Lectures. **Hewitt Lectures.**
Carpentier Lectures. **Jesup Lectures.**

Catalogues will be sent free on application.

THE MACMILLAN COMPANY, AGENTS

64-66 FIFTH AVENUE, NEW YORK

THE COLUMBIA UNIVERSITY PRESS

Columbia University in the City of New York

Books published at net *prices are sold by booksellers everywhere at the advertised* net *prices. When delivered from the publishers, carriage, either postage or expressage, is an extra charge.*

COLUMBIA UNIVERSITY LECTURES

BLUMENTHAL LECTURES

POLITICAL PROBLEMS OF AMERICAN DEVELOPMENT. By ALBERT SHAW, LL.D., Editor of the *Review of Reviews.* 12mo, cloth, pp. vii + 268. Price, $1.50 *net.*

CONSTITUTIONAL GOVERNMENT IN THE UNITED STATES. By WOODROW WILSON, LL.D., President of Princeton University. 12mo, cloth, pp. vii + 236. Price, $1.50 *net.*

THE PRINCIPLES OF POLITICS FROM THE VIEWPOINT OF THE AMERICAN CITIZEN. By JEREMIAH W. JENKS, LL.D., Professor of Political Economy and Politics in Cornell University. 12mo, cloth, pp. xviii + 187. Price, $1.50 *net.*

HEWITT LECTURES

THE PROBLEM OF MONOPOLY. A Study of a Grave Danger and the Means of Averting it. By JOHN BATES CLARK, LL.D., Professor of Political Economy, Columbia University. 12mo, cloth, pp. vi + 128. Price, $1.25 *net.*

JESUP LECTURES

LIGHT. By RICHARD C. MACLAURIN, LL.D., Sc.D., President of the Massachusetts Institute of Technology. 12mo, cloth, pp. ix + 251. Price, $1.50 *net.*

THE MACMILLAN COMPANY, AGENTS

64-66 FIFTH AVENUE, NEW YORK

Bei Fragen zur Produktsicherheit wenden Sie sich bitte an:
If you have any questions regarding product safety,
please contact:

Walter de Gruyter GmbH
Genthiner Straße 13
10785 Berlin
productsafety@degruyterbrill.com